The Limoges Porcelain Box

THE LIMOGES PORCELAIN BOX

from *Snuff*  to *Sentiments*

Text by Joanne Furio
Photography by George Ross and Freddy Le Saux

All inquiries should be addressed to:
Lake Warren Press, 135 West 26th Street, New York, NY 10001
telephone: 212.679.4615

Library of Congress Catalogue Card Number: 98-66712
ISBN: 0-9664817-0-4

Produced by Lake Isle Press, Inc.
Project Editor: Clover Archer
Book Design: Liz Trovato

Printed in Hong Kong

September 1998
First Edition

DEDICATION

To the memory of Liliane Fouquet,
my creative partner and friend, and all of the other wonderful people past
and present who have contributed to making these tiny boxes
such a large part of so many lives.

Foreword

I became a collector at an early age. In the mid-1950s, when I was about 7 or 8, I had quite a collection of Match Box cars. I remember being perfectly content to play with them for hours, spinning the wheels and admiring the tiny strokes of pinstriping. I cherished this collection and to my mind, it was a most impressive and comprehensive assortment.

For Christmas one year, while many boys were opening up big, shiny Lionel trains, I was busy piecing together my new HO set, about a third the size of Lionel. In retrospect, I'm still not sure if I received the HO set by happenstance or if my parents had sensed my fascination with small things and intended to nurture it. Nevertheless, that train set further enhanced my fascination with intricately detailed miniatures.

The summer of 1964 was spent with my best friend, Gene Agatstein, riding bikes and looking for discarded soda cans—not to redeem but to create "shorties," a perfect-looking can half the size of a regular one. To make a shortie, you had to meticulously bend and cut the cans in half (without the aid of hand tools) and stuff half the can inside the other. The cut seam had to be even and flush to the rim of the other half. If we did it right—presto! We had a perfectly proportioned, half-sized can to admire and collect. By the end of that summer a shelf running the length of the wall above Gene's bed featured our creations: hundreds of shorties stacked perfectly to form a pyramid. And it was perfect—until the shelf came crashing down in the middle of the night. It was a good choice to have kept them at Gene's.

Looking back at my tendency to collect and my attraction to small things, it seems perfectly appropriate that I would spend my adult life buying, selling and collecting tiny handmade, hand-painted porcelain boxes. Their appeal is undeniable: each shape painted to create a perfect little box, many too small to hold anything, but each so beautifully complete by itself and somehow equally as beautiful when clustered with other shapes. It has never been a surprise to me that so many people would be as mesmerized with these boxes as I have been.

This book was conceived for all the collectors who visit these boxes often, opening them, holding them and constantly admiring their miniature beauty. For those who may wonder, "Why the fascination?", there is good reason. Each box has a sense of history. Open a box and you can feel it. Now I hope you will enjoy reading about it.

Initially I wanted to document only the historical significance of the *tabatière*, a specific, though limited look back to 17th- and 18th-century Europe. Tracing the *tabatière* is, in effect, tracing a slice of European history. The entire social structure was represented in the making of porcelain *tabatières*—from the craftsmen who created them to the royalty who commissioned and collected them. As in art, the porcelain *tabatière* mirrored the prevailing attitudes of the time, reflecting the lavish lifestyle in France. The porcelain box became yet another medium, a canvas to reflect art for many to collect and appreciate.

But writing about history alone would have told only part of the story. I also wanted to let collectors know about Rochard's involvement in the development of these boxes, the creative process involved and the painstaking steps taken to create these tiny works of art—past and present. In many ways very little has changed. The creative process hasn't changed with time. Perhaps techniques change, styles change, but the process, by and large, has endured. I consider myself most fortunate indeed to be part of this process, working with very creative and talented artists on this ancient art form.

Over the past two decades the popularity of Limoges porcelain boxes has soared. Over the years I have spoken to many who share my passion for these tiny objects, some with collections totaling hundreds, others who are beginners with one or two pieces. Whether one has an entire cabinet to display his or her collection or a sole box on a table or mantel, the one thing all collectors share is the passionate way they describe their Rochard boxes—in great detail, from the shape, to the painting with so many colors, to the design of the clasp where it opens to what's inside. Nothing is missed. It's quite gratifying to know that all the time and effort spent conceiving, constructing and designing each piece is recognized, appreciated and enjoyed.

I will forever remember sitting with Robert Piotet and seeing the first of a series of animal boxes, each shiny and smooth. The graceful pheasant with its long flowing tail and so many wonderful colors. Every time I studied it I would see new colors and new details. I think of working with Liliane Fouquet, a woman who started her business in the basement of her home. She had a collection of no more than 15 porcelain boxes: a small rooster, two lovebirds facing each other and the rest traditional shapes of hearts, chests and eggs. We both felt the same enthusiasm and encouraged each other to reproduce antique shapes and to create new ones. Madame Fouquet's energy and inspiration have been instrumental in my life.

I have been fortunate to have worked with Monsieur Piotet; Madame Fouquet; Henri Parry; Guy Vieille; Antonio Diez; Jean-Luc Soulat; Joseph Oliveira; Maryvonne Esnaud; Jean-Claude Cubaut; Lionel Marcolini; Jean-Paul Marquet; Patrice Fiorucci; Alain Caillot; Christophe Escure; Didier and Paulette Destieux; Jean-Jacques and Maria Goy; Gérard and Mady Chastagner; and the Ribierre family. I have always been impressed with each and everyone's creative contribution, uncompromising attention to detail and unwavering desire to create not only something that would sell but something very special.

Because of this, all collectors (myself included) can look forward to the future, the new shapes and designs, the possibilities. We will add to our collections, move them around, rearrange the groupings, position the most recent box with the first and constantly marvel at their beauty. After all, isn't that what collecting is all about?

RICHARD SONKING

Contents

Introduction

A beautiful Limoges porcelain box. Easily held in the palm of one's hand, it is the epitome of miniature beauty, of craftsmanship par excellence. When admiring these miniatures, it may be difficult, in this day and age, to imagine the colorful history behind these highly collectible objets d'art. Remarkably, they were at once objects of contempt—Louis XIV abhorred snuff—and desire—one German count possessed more than 700 of them.

To understand the origins of today's Limoges porcelain box, one has to consider both the history of porcelain, to discover how Limoges became a world leader in producing fine porcelain, and the snuff boxes of the late- 17th and 18th- centuries, when many of the designs that continue to inspire designers today were first created by French factories.

Looking back, it is amazing to discover that very little has changed in the manufacturing of these boxes in the 300 years since their introduction. The process continues to be done by hand and in miniature. Today's boxes, however, serve a more decorative, sentimental purpose.

Originally created to hold snuff, but also candies and other cherished objects, these miniature boxes became symbols of their times, reflecting, perhaps more than any other everyday object, the social mores, decorative skills, technological advances and even the politics of the ancien régime. Today, Limoges boxes are used to mark life's special occasions or are collected as objects of lasting beauty. A mere box? Not quite. The decorative objects we collect today provide us with a clear and colorful link to the past—and the creative possibilities of tomorrow.

In the Beginning

After his historic 24-year trip to the Orient, Marco Polo dictated a book to a popular writer on all that he had seen and heard in his travels. Among the many items that inspired awe, fascination and wonder in the eyes of this great explorer were Chinese ceramics with a luminous, brilliant white surface he compared to the marine mollusk called *porcella* in Italian. Europeans unfamiliar with Chinese porcelain confused it with a type of mother of pearl made from the mollusk's iridescent, internal surface called *porcellana* (or *porcelaine* in French), which they believed possessed certain magic properties.

When kneaded together with plaster and eggs, this mollusk mixture was used to create beautiful objects. According to the Italian scholar Guido Panciroli, the concoction was to be hidden in the ground by the head of the family and remain there for 80 years "without being brought to the light." Once removed, it had to be fashioned "into those precious vases, so beautiful to the eye in shape and color that architects cannot detect any defect in them." Such vases were believed to have such powerful properties that if poison were put into them they would immediately "burst asunder." He who buried this material would never see it again—it was left for his children or other heirs, hoping they would derive benefits from it, since it was considered more valuable than gold.

The Chinese, so renowned for their porcelain-making, influenced European style and decoration for centuries. This soft-paste porcelain snuffbox was made at Saint-Cloud in 1750.

Marco Polo arrives in China, where he will befriend kings, discover silk, jade, ivory and a luminous, brilliant-white ceramic that becomes known as porcelain (right).

Even though what Polo brought back was a material quite unlike this primitive mix, medieval Europeans nevertheless bestowed its superstitions upon porcelain and avoided it at all costs. In fact, some historians believe that it probably took so long for Europe to discover porcelain because it had been impeded by such supernatural beliefs. According to French porcelain expert Edouard Garnier, "such absurd tales" were even believed by the most learned men and were still seriously told during the second half of the 17th century. So it could be said that Polo, while credited with bringing ivory, jade, silk and the idea of paper money to the West, by giving porcelain its name, inadvertently contributed to the confusion over its meaning.

And so we begin the tale of porcelain, whose early history is riddled with much controversy and contradiction. The Polo story, for example, is but one of several describing the naming of porcelain. Another credits the Portuguese who, along with the Venetians, are considered to be among the first to bring Chinese porcelain to Europe during the Middle Ages. It's easy to see how the Portuguese were contenders—their word for a certain marine mollusk is *porcullana*.

Whether it was the Venetians, the Portuguese or Marco Polo who were responsible for naming porcelain, one thing is certain: Polo is the one who opened up trade between East and West on a grand scale and therefore is often credited with popularizing the precious objects a century later. From that moment on, craftsmen all over Europe were scurrying to copy the unique characteristics of that luminous, precious material from the Far East they simply referred to as "china."

The Secret from China

TIMELINE:

620 A.D.
T'ang Dynasty: Chinese begin making hard-paste porcelain.

1100s
European traders first bring porcelain to Europe.

1296
Marco Polo returns to Italy after his historic trip to China, bringing back larger quantities of porcelain.

1520
First Chinese porcelains imported to the West.

1602
Dutch East India Company begins importing porcelain from Asia to Europe.

1720
Dutch East India Company imports of Oriental porcelain reach their peak.

Because of its preciousness, only the very rich, i.e., nobility, were able to collect the real thing. Beginning what was to become a longstanding tradition among the rich and powerful, the first piece of porcelain listed in a European inventory—a jug from the Yuan period (1271–1368) was a gift, from Louis I, King of Hungary, to Charles III of Durazzo (Hungary) in 1382. King Francis I and Emperor Charles V, both of France, and the Medicis of Italy all collected porcelain. Records show that Ming porcelains were ordered by King Manoel of Portugal and Emperor Charles V, who possessed the earliest surviving dinner service, decorated with his coat of arms. Tableware became a staple of porcelain production from the very beginning because the rich, just like everyone else, wanted to put out their best for guests.

What set porcelain apart from other types of ceramics, and what inspired Polo to make his comparison to *porcella*, was the luminosity of these objects. Unlike the heavier, thicker ceramics being made by Europeans, Chinese porcelain had a lightness and transparency that both dazzled and defied the best European potters.

The Chinese had known the secret to making porcelain since the T'ang Dynasty (618–907). There, it had occupied a place of honor within the society. Lovely to look at, delightful to touch, it even made a pleasant sound. So treasured, it was used as a surface on which poetry was inscribed. Chinese emperors were so enamored with this precious material, they ordered the creation of royal factories during the Sung dynasty (960–1279) so they could decorate their palaces with porcelain objects. The Chinese remained the undisputed masters of porcelain manufacturing for centuries. During the Ming dynasty (1368–1644), which many collectors believe to be a highpoint in porcelain artistry, porcelain makers perfected a famous blue and white underglaze.

The secret of making porcelain had spread to Korea in the 1100s and to Japan in the 1500s. When traders brought these exotic items back to Europe in the 1100s, the European aristocracy immediately responded to their aesthetic beauty and porcelain quickly became one of the most important exports from China.

THE SINCEREST FORM OF FLATTERY

By the beginning of the 17th century, China was enjoying a long era of unprecedented prosperity and Chinese porcelain-making reached its peak, in technique, variety of materials and above all, decoration. Not surprisingly, the European demand for such beautiful objects reached fantastic proportions and the trade gap between China and Europe grew even larger.

One of the largest importers of Chinese porcelain was the Dutch East India Company, which in 1602 had been granted a monopoly by the Dutch government to import goods from Asia to the Netherlands. In addition to selling porcelain to other European markets, the Dutch loved porcelain themselves and their favorite pattern was the blue-and-white motif, which made its first appearance in China in 1279 and would dominate the Chinese export market by the 16th and 17th centuries.

Indeed, the Dutch so revered these objects that they were included in still-life painting; and the Dutch also provided the Chinese with the sincerest form of flattery—imitation. In Delft, ceramicists created two-toned earthenware inspired by the Chinese, which remained popular for many decades. But the Dutch copies were often inferior to the Oriental because they lacked not only the technical skill of the Far East painters, but the actual raw material itself—the elusive porcelain. In fact, Europeans believed this special clay could only be found in the East. Lacking "the Chinese secret," European potters were resigned to imitating the look however they could.

Delft craftsmen used a lead glaze, made white and opaque with the addition of tin oxide to a lightly fired earthenware body, which they then decorated with a metallic oxide of cobalt. In actuality, this was no porcelain but instead a type of faïence, or tin-glazed earthenware (see page 21). Such imitations were further enhanced by a clear lead glaze that sought to complete the illusion.

By the beginning of the 18th century, the Dutch East India company was importing whole shipments of china from the East, in addition to bringing silk and teas into the homes of Europeans. By the 1720s, Dutch East India ships were carrying as many as 200,000 pieces of porcelain. In such times, when the wealth of a nation was determined solely by its natural resources and its ability to turn them into precious commodities, it was one raw material that separated East and West. Little did the Europeans know, this raw material would be found in their own backyards.

THE SECRET INGREDIENT

The missing ingredient was kaolin, a white infusible clay that is a silicate of aluminum, which creates the so-called "hard-paste" porcelain (see page 21). Europeans were so far from thinking that this material could be found in the earth that alchemists alone were set to search for its manufacturing secret and make it themselves. Without kaolin, Europeans were forced to create a soft-paste or artificial porcelain, a substitute more like glass.

Soft-paste or *artificial porcelain* had a much more porous texture that was irregular, grainy and stained from use. In contrast, *hard-paste porcelain*, what we today know as porcelain, tends to be whiter, finer and has a shinier, more polished look when painted.

Such dazzling examples of porcelain arriving from the Far East must have frustrated and taunted European craftsmen even more. Aware of the amount of porcelain being exported into their countries, both Louis XIV of France, known as the "Sun King" for choosing the sun as his royal emblem, and August II, "Augustus the Strong," the Elector of Saxony (what is today Germany) and King of Poland, began a technological race to discover the secret behind Chinese porcelain. Their intentions were two fold: not only did they want to correct the trade imbalance, they were also very fond of this coveted ware themselves.

In the end it was Germany that would win the race to discover the secret of Chinese porcelain—but it would be by chance rather than by calculation. Augustus had happened to imprison a young alchemist, Johann Friedrich Böttger, who was obsessed with the idea of finding the Philosopher's Stone. If Böttger were successful, the king wanted complete control of the windfall, so the king ordered him to make gold—or else. As fate would have it, Böttger was ordered to work with Ehrenfried von Tschirnhausen, an experienced chemist and physicist who had been working on an inventory of all minerals to be found in Saxony, subjecting them to high temperatures in an attempt to make silver synthetically. Instead of making gold or silver, the two would discover how to make hard-paste porcelain.

When it was clear that Böttger's attempts to turn base metals into gold would prove futile, he suggested instead that the two begin to look for the secret ingredient of Chinese porcelain. Augustus, temporarily appeased by the thought of squeezing taxes from a new industry, agreed to put on hold his gold-making venture.

The exact date of the discovery of porcelain in Europe is not known. It had been kept a dark and mysterious secret, but it was likely between late 1708 or early 1709. So momentous was this discovery, it was considered a state secret and actually caused a number of industrial spy intrigues. Legend has it that this "multipurpose natural resource" was being used to powder wigs and that Böttger discovered it one morning when he found his wig to be heavier than usual. At any rate, on March 20, 1709, Böttger announced to the king that he was able to make porcelain "in such perfection as to be equal to if not surpass the East Indian" and presented him with the first object made in European hard-

The Discovery of Kaolin in Germany

TIMELINE:

1708–09
Böttger and von Tschirnhausen discover kaolin.

1710
First object made of European hard-paste porcelain.

*A barrel-shaped
double box decorated with flowers
(Meissen, circa 1750–1755).*

paste porcelain. A year later, in the Albrechtsburg fortress at Meissen, the very fortress where Böttger had been imprisoned, the Royal Saxon Porcelain Manufactory was established on January 23. Four years later, Böttger, a heavy drinker, died at the age of 37. Tschirnhausen had died in October 1708, unable to celebrate the fruit of his labors. And history would unfairly give Böttger full credit for the discovery of kaolin.

THE MEISSEN ROYAL MANUFACTORY

The success of the Meissen factory was rapid. Collectors immediately recognized the high quality of Meissen porcelain and it quickly dampened the Chinese export market. From that moment on, China would no longer set the standard, but it would continue to provide a strong design influence during this time of great exploration and colonization, when the exotic and foreign were highly romanticized by the European style setters.

For the Meissen artisans, pleasing the whims of an aristocratic clientele was not easy, but they could not fail by first producing lavish table services and vases, which became the rage of foreign courts. Beginning in 1727, sculptors were summoned there to try their skills on this newly emerging art form. One of the most well-known of them, Joachim Kandler, created small porcelain statuary

of allegorical or mythological figures or characters from the commedia dell'arte, combining realistic expression with an appealing palette. These figures became very much in demand in Europe and were frequently imitated. The sculptor's workshop also referred to botanical manuals to produce painted floral decorations that were known for their realism.

At the request of Augustus, who sought imposing decorations to help furnish his palace, the factory produced a zoo of some of the finest large porcelain animals ever made. Because of their size, and since they often required double firings because of their enamel decorations, the large animals were extremely difficult to make. As a result, some were left white or painted with unfired colors, which have mostly worn away. One of these animals, the Bolognese hound, is on display at the Metropolitan Museum of Art in New York. It is believed to be the work of J. G. Kirchner, a sculptor who worked with Kandler until 1733.

By the mid-18th century, Meissen had become the leading European porcelain factory—to the chagrin of the French and other European ceramicists, who also had to contend with high-quality imports from yet another source. Unfortunately for the French, the discovery of kaolin on their soil would not be for another 55 years after the German find.

What's What: Differentiating Ceramics

The best artisans may try to fool you, but if you look carefully, you can probably distinguish between the many types of ceramics, a category that includes all types of heat-hardened clay objects:

EARTHENWARE: The earliest human handicraft, dating to Neolithic times. Made by firing at a low temperature, earthenware includes any clay form that is porous. It may or may not be treated with a glaze.

STONEWARE: a nonporous material without glazing, it is fired at a high temperature, producing objects that are very dense and heavy.

FAÏENCE: Earthenware with a white tin-based glaze, often decorated with hand-painted motifs. Some French artisans of the mid-17th century who believed they were creating soft-paste porcelain were in fact creating a type of faïence.

DELFT: A type of faïence created by the Dutch, in the city of Delft, beginning in the 17th century. Typically blue and white, this motif was copied from Chinese patterns that originated in the 13th century.

SOFT-PASTE OR ARTIFICIAL PORCELAIN: First invented in Florence during the second half of the 16th century, soft-paste porcelain was used by French ceramicists until the end of the 18th century. Made from a combination of materials, including white clay, which made the paste opaque, and other glasslike substances, soft-paste porcelain was fired at a lower temperature than hard-paste porcelain, and therefore never fully vitrified—it remained somewhat porous. The finished product had an irregular, grainy texture that stained with use. As a result, it did not hold paints as well as its hard-paste counterpart. Soft-paste porcelain has a creamier tone than hard-paste porcelain, and when decorated, the colors merge with the glaze to create a softer effect.

HARD-PASTE PORCELAIN: Also called true porcelain or natural porcelain, hard-paste porcelain was first discovered by the Chinese, then, 1,000 years later, by the Europeans, and is what we today consider to be porcelain. Made from kaolin, a white clay that is mined from the earth, mixed with petunse, a type of feldspar, and quartz (see photo above), hard-paste porcelain has a smooth surface achieved by the fusion of body and glaze under a very high firing. It is that complete fusion of clay and glaze that creates the luminescence for which porcelain is so noted. Breaking a piece of such porcelain would reveal no difference between body and glaze. Hard-paste porcelain tends to be whiter, finer and has a shinier, more polished look when painted.

BONE CHINA: A technique created by the English in the 1750s, bone china is basically made by adding bone ash (burned animal bones) to the porcelain mixture, greatly increasing the translucence of the finished product. Such products are not as hard as hard-paste porcelain, but are more durable than soft-paste wares. Today, England remains the world's largest producer of bone china.

In the absence of the ingredient that created the luminous, hard-wearing porcelain, Europeans had no other choice but to continue to use soft-paste porcelain. Importing kaolin from Germany—or even China—was out of the question. It was much too costly and the Germans would not have parted with it anyway since they wanted it for their own factories. So the French, along with other European potters who had not yet discovered kaolin on their own soil, continued to use soft-paste porcelain, which the French called *pâte tendre*, the "French porcelain par excellence," and made the best of their situation.

The absence of hard-paste porcelain seemed to have no effect on French creativity or design. After all, the French had a long history of pottery-making, with each porcelain workshop possessing its own secret processes and skills. Since each porcelain piece was considered a work of art, it was never produced in batches. Instead, porcelain production resembled an interesting experiment, with perfection being the goal.

Even though the Asian and Meissen porcelain continued to set the technological standard, French soft-paste porcelain wares still made their distinctive mark. While it's true that Oriental porcelain was often copied by the French (as well as the Germans), the result was not a slavish copy, but chinoiserie, which mimics the Asian but is made distinctly European by the use of certain motifs and painting techniques. Each factory was highly individualized: each had its own signature look and its own

Soft-Paste Porcelain Factories in France

TIMELINE:

1664
Patent for porcelain-making granted to Claude and François Révérent, at Saint-Cloud, who were in fact making faïence.

1667
Pierre Chicaneau claims to make the first soft-paste porcelain in France at Saint-Cloud.

1673
Louis Poterat granted patent for porcelain-making. It is believed he was making faïence at this point.

1690
Poterat makes first soft-paste pieces at Rouen.

specialties—even if it shared some of the same objects and, at times, the same employees, who moved from factory to factory, taking snippets of vital technical information along with them.

Tableware, a staple of porcelain production, was always in steady demand. Some factories produced a variety of common everyday objects, including knife handles, walking stick knobs and cups, which were not as decorative as statuary or as coveted as a snuffbox.

PROTECTION FROM THE RULING CLASS

The difficulty that all factories shared was in being successful as commercial enterprises. Compared to other types of ceramics, porcelain required firings at higher temperatures, which meant more wood for the kilns, and the repeated firings created more risk of breakage. Losses were high, and many entrepreneurs failed. Those who were successful had to seek the patronage of royalty, mostly dukes or princes, who would bestow protections upon the factories. These edicts were nothing more than privileges that sought to create monopolies to stifle the competition. Louis Poterat, for example, was granted an exclusive right to manufacture porcelain for all of Normandy. And only one factory, Vincennes-Sèvres, had the protection of the king and was therefore elevated to the highest rank. Among the many protections, the one that proved most stifling was the prohibition that banned other factories from making gilt-trimmed wares, a rule that history demonstrates was broken several times. Manufacturers, except for "La Manufacture Royale," were also hindered by a heavy transportation tax, which increased their costs substantially. At the very least, these protections, by imposing certain restrictions, seem to have created a system of specialization that encouraged factories to explore other creative venues.

Factory owners also scurried for protection from nobles because they knew the nobles had a keen interest in supporting art and industry and enjoyed the benefits of being patrons. It was a status symbol to be able to have objects created with one's own special seal, and to one's specifications. Despite complaints from the factory managers, enforcement of these rules was not taken seriously by bureaucrats. Perhaps they realized that in the long run, conflicts would boil down to a battle of wills, pitting one royal against another. Nevertheless, competition was fierce: each manufacturer sought to create work of the highest quality, steal the discoveries of one another and lure their competitors' finest craftsmen.

AND THE REAL INVENTOR IS...

Even though soft-paste porcelain was not as coveted as hard paste, its history is nevertheless as riddled with contradictions as the history of hard-paste porcelain. Many, it seems, boasted that they had discovered the secret of hard-paste porcelain, which, of course, they hadn't.

Still others tried to take credit for discovering soft-paste porcelain, but may have been making a type of faïence instead. A case in point: in 1664 a privilege or patent for "porcelain-making" was granted to Claude and François Révérend in Saint-Cloud, but it is believed that there was confusion over the meaning of the word and that they had instead been making faïence.

ROUEN (1673–96)

Another porcelain patent was granted in 1673 to Louis Poterat, master of the faïence manufactory of Rouen. In 1690 he is mentioned in the first record of porcelain manufacturing of France as having "found the secret of making porcelain objects in France." When his faïence privilege was up for renewal in 1694, the question of his porcelain was taken up by the authorities. It seems Poterat had indeed created a few soft-paste porcelain pieces, but clandestinely, so his workers wouldn't sell his secret to rivals.

The earliest porcelains at Rouen took their forms from the art of gold- and silversmiths. These simple shapes became vases, cups and saucers without handles. (Handles had been too difficult to affix and were therefore eliminated.) Complex shapes were avoided and, generally, colorings were blue and white. There are few examples that exist today.

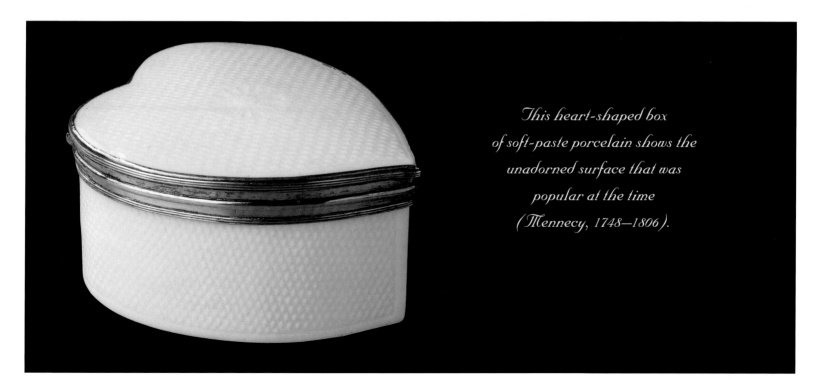

This heart-shaped box of soft-paste porcelain shows the unadorned surface that was popular at the time (Mennecy, 1748–1806).

SAINT-CLOUD (1678–1766)

Whiteware from this factory was so much an improvement over Rouen's, some have actually credited its founder, Pierre Chicaneau, a colleague of Poterat's, with the discovery of soft-paste porcelain in about 1667. He, too, claimed to have made "true porcelain" by producing "pieces almost as perfect as the porcelains of China..." Chicaneau died in 1678, and the following year his widow married Henri-Charles Trou, who secured for the factory the protection of the Duc d'Orléans. Strangely enough, it appears that Trou never learned how to manufacture soft-paste porcelain, which the factory claimed to have perfected in 1693. When his wife died in 1722, a renewed patent was taken out by Trou's son, Henri II, and the factory remained in the family until 1766, when it went into bankruptcy.

No matter what its origins, one thing is certain about Saint-Cloud porcelain—its products did represent a vast improvement in technical craft. (To today's eye, however, they appear quite crude, even

folksy.) A famous English doctor, writing in a travel book, was so moved as to describe Saint-Cloud porcelain "as a great good fortune of our times to equal, or even to surpass, the Chinese in their most beautiful art."

Saint-Cloud porcelain is a warm ivory color—some might even say yellow-tinged—with a glassy glaze and minute surface pitting. Objects from Saint-Cloud can often be identified by their colorings: the blues tended to be runny, the yellow of a burnt shade, and the reds were used to outline.

Saint-Cloud first produced small, Chinese-style objects in blue and white or white alone, which were gradually abandoned, giving way to more varied decoration. Most of the objects were tableware and vases, which again imitated Chinese style or Japanese porcelain in the Imari tradition, a pictorial style developed in the Kyushu region of Japan, but the high baroque was soon adopted (see page 68 for definitions).

The Saint-Cloud factory was known for its Chinese-inspired objects (see above), especially its collection of animals. A Saint-Cloud cat from 1735, pictured at the right, inspired Rochard's contemporary version (left).

CHANTILLY (1725–1800)

Louis Henri, the Duc de Condé and a part-time chemist with a passion for collecting porcelain (at his death an inventory lists 2,000 pieces), founded a manufactory at his château in Chantilly in 1725 with the help of one Ciquaire Cirous. During the factory's first 25 years, when many believe its best porcelain was made, tin oxide was often added to the glaze to give the appearance of hard porcelain. The first wares were pure white, but later many were inspired by the Japanese Kakiemon style, which depicted simple themes, such as a dragon, on a white background. Their simplicity set them apart from the rococo taste that was emerging at the time. Other Oriental patterns, naturalistic in style, following a trend set by Meissen, were also produced here.

The duke became very involved in design and development. His wealth had enabled him to accumulate a vast collection of Oriental porcelains, which he encouraged his craftsmen to copy.

At parties in his home, he took much delight in asking guests which objects were the imitations and which were the Asian originals.

Eventually, chinoiserie gave way to more European designs. Chinese figures were replaced by more Western-looking ones; flowers of European gardens, most notably pansies, began to mix with the Asian. From 1760–76 the design had become purely European, with floral decorations, landscapes and love scenes imitating the French court painter François Boucher (see page 74). Tableware formed the major part of the production. Animal forms appeared as small toys or *bonbonnières*, containers for bite-sized chocolates called bonbons.

After the Revolution, an Englishman named Potter tried to revive the factory, but his and about half a dozen other attempts failed. Chantilly continued to produce porcelain off and on, after a long succession of proprietors, until about 1800.

*A delicately painted
18th century soft-paste porcelain box
from Chantilly (above).*

*A Chantilly box from 1740
in the form of a sleeping couple provided the
inspiration for a popular Rochard box
(right) called "Mr. and Mrs. St. Denis."*

MENNECY-VILLEROY (1748–1806)

First established in Paris by François Barbin on the Rue de Charonne, the factory was granted the protection of the Duc de Villeroy in 1734 and transferred to Mennecy in 1748. In 1773 it was again transferred, this time to Bourg-la-Reine, where it remained until closing its doors.

Under the direction of the brothers Robert and Gilles Dubois, efforts were made to break from the Oriental style and produce porcelain similar to Meissen. Ironically, Meissen factories themselves were imitating Oriental porcelain.

The Dubois brothers, talented though they were, have become the history of porcelain's most ubiquitous characters, hopping from factory to factory, accumulating precious technical information along the way. Boastful and brazen, they were first employed at Chantilly, where they claimed to learn the secret of porcelain-making.

Under their leadership, Mennecy nonetheless managed to distinguish itself by producing porcelain wares of a purple-red and a thick enamel-like application of blues, reds and yellows. In its last years, cream-colored earthenware, similar to that made popular by Josiah Wedgwood, was produced. Although Mennecy did produce a milky-white porcelain with a brilliant glaze, the tough monopolies granted to Vincennes and Sèvres prohibited them from adding a gold border. Figurines were also made at Mennecy, including groups of children, and fruit and animals in the form of snuffboxes.

Many of the snuffboxes made at Mennecy were in the form of animals, such as this horse (circa 1760, above), which was the inspiration for the contemporary piece (left).

Eighteenth-century snuffboxes, such as this graceful swan (circa 1750–60, right), were often made to fit comfortably in the palm of one's hand.

VINCENNES (1738–1756) SÈVRES (1756–PRESENT)

The Dubois brothers eventually founded the Vincennes factory. The two won the favor of the Comptroller General Orry de Vignory, who financed their attempts with help from the king. De Vignory had the brothers set up shop at the Château de Vincennes, a royal property, and secured a sizable advance of capital for them in about 1738. Unfortunately for the brothers, their porcelain failed to meet expectations and they were dismissed in 1741.

The venture continued with the help of yet another Chantilly deserter, François Gravant, who was a bit more successful than the Dubois siblings. In 1745 a good soft-paste porcelain was produced and in 1751, the Marquise de Pompadour, a mistress of Louis XV famous for her extravagant taste, persuaded the king to subsidize the factory. In 1753 Vincennes received the title "Manufacture Royale" and was given permission to mark its products with Louis XV's two interlaced Ls.

This first privilege of many to be granted attempted to eliminate competition from other French manufacturers by prohibiting them, for a period of 20 years, from manufacturing porcelain in the "style of Saxon" (meaning Meissen), which in this particular case meant gilded. Another privilege prohibited other factories from hiring Vincennes-Sèvres workers. (The latter seems to have been ignored more than the first.) Yet another privilege levied a transportation tax on porcelain factories, except the Manufacture Royale.

In 1756 the Vincennes workshop moved to Sèvres, between Paris and Versailles, and within four years went bankrupt, becoming the sole property of the king.

After the discovery of kaolin in France in 1769, the factory began making hard-paste porcelain and continued to create soft-paste porcelain; the number of workers grew to 274 in 1783. Soft-paste porcelain was completely eliminated around 1800, when Alexandre Brongniart, appointed by Napoleon to take over the administration of Sèvres, deemed it too costly.

Even though its charter states that Vincennes would set out to imitate the quality and excellence of Meissen, that promise quickly faded and Vincennes-Sèvres developed a style of its own. As a royal manufactory, serving the whims and wishes of the King and his court at Versailles, Sèvres achieved excellence in craftsmanship and elegance of design, attracting the world's best artisans and painters.

Louis XV took a personal interest in the factory and used table services from Sèvres as gifts to other European sovereigns. Many of the designs were quite imaginative using wreaths, intertwined motifs and lively borders. Decoration under his successor, Louis XVI, as if sensing the political upheaval to come, became more subdued

On the eve of the Revolution, Louis XVI, noting that the privileges accorded to Sèvres were now an object of ridicule, agreed to make the manufactory a kind of laboratory that would serve as a model to other French factories by producing the finest porcelain in France. Though politically motivated, the designation was not without its merits.

Sèvres paste was known for its purity and its painters had achieved national notoriety. As a result, Sèvres became famous the world over for its superior tableware and for the quality of its gilding, taught at great expense by a Benedictine Monk. Early works, influenced by the Chantilly workers, were in the Kakiemon style. Larger and often highly decorated vases followed, as well as sculpture often mounted on gold or silver bases. Tableware was abundant and included goblets, sugar bowls, teapots, cups and saucers, fruit dishes, bowls, plates, oil pots, salt cellars, etc. Toilette items included shaving bowls, rouge pots and sponge boxes.

In about 1753 it became fashionable at Sèvres to leave figures in the *'biscuit,'* or unglazed, a fashion that has continued until the present day.

A Rochard tea warmer (above).

Interlaced Ls, ⚭, which manufacturers used well into the 20th century, are on the bottom of this Limoges porcelain powder box circa 1925. (Private collection of Gérard Ribierre)

The French Discover Kaolin

Timeline:

1764
Madame Darnet discovers kaolin in Saint Yrieix.

1769
Discovery of French porcelain confirmed after repeated experiments. First hard-paste porcelain pieces from Limoges kaolin are manufactured at Manufacture Royale de Sèvres.

The French were aware that the absence of kaolin was a technological drawback, but they didn't seriously look for it on their own soil until the early 1760s. As fate would have it, kaolin was not found by a geologist or a chemist, but a housewife—or so the story goes . . .

One day in 1764 or thereabouts, while washing her clothing in a nearby stream, Madame Darnet, a surgeon's wife in the village of Saint Yrieix, about 40 kilometers (about 25 miles) from Limoges, ran out of bleaching powder. Inadvertently, she made use of a white unctuous clay she found in a nearby ravine. (Some versions of the legend say she had been using this clay as a detergent for quite some time.) When she showed the white clay to her husband, he quickly had it sent to an apothecary in Bordeaux who recognized it to be kaolin. Samples were then sent to the chemist Macquer of Sèvres. He went to Saint Yrieix in August of 1768, and after years of repeated experiments, presented a formal paper in June of 1769 on the discovery of French hard porcelain.

Unfortunately for Madame Darnet, some would actually credit Monsieur Darnet with the discovery of French kaolin, perhaps because he was the more prominent and had actually been involved in getting the substance to the lab. Most historical accounts, however, credit his wife.

Giddy with the discovery, and the prospect of becoming rich through hardly any effort at all, residents of Saint Yrieix began digging up their properties and selling kaolin. Some, like Jean-Baptiste Joseph Garreau, the Comte de la Seynie, witnessing the success of factories elsewhere, decided to sell the kaolin and set up a factory. Soon, Saint Yrieix was humming with commercial activity and the promise of a prosperous future.

King Louis XV, still basking in the glow of his predecessor, and Anne Robert Jacques Turgot, the governor of the province of Limousin, which included Limoges and St. Yrieix, quickly realized the significance of the discovery. The French would now be able to enjoy the most luxurious of ceramics and stop the flow of expensive imports. Turgot wanted to keep this new material, and the new wealth it would create, within the borders of the Limousin.

A miner transports kaolin from the mine in a basket on his head.

An anonymous portrait of Monsieur Darnet, credited with discovering French kaolin. Legend has it, however, that it was his wife who stumbled upon the clay while washing clothes.

Limoges

Looking back at Limoges's history, one can appreciate how this industrialized city in the rocky, wooded hills of the French countryside was poised to become synonymous with fine porcelain. Limoges had been a crossroads for travelers, a hub of commerce and a center for fine craftsmanship from its very beginnings. As early as 3,000 years before Christ, pottery was being produced in the region.

What we now call Limoges was originally Augustoritum, a Gallo-Roman settlement first described in the early second century, located near a bridge on the River Vienne where two Roman roads converged. The Limousin was then populated by the Gallic tribe of the Lemovices who renamed the settlement after themselves. After the fall of the Roman Empire, Limoges became a large and important city under the Merovingians and Carolingians, as well as an artistic and commercial center of coin minting, gold- and silversmithing and enameling. Eventually Limoges would develop into two separate cities with distinct ideological and economic differences.

One was called La Cité, after the Roman *Civitas*, and presided over by the bishop of Limoges. By the 7th century, another settlement called Le Château, named after the home of its viscount, was founded and developed much more rapidly. Le Château had numerous open spaces that served as markets and was fiercely democratic. La Cité had four churches, four convents, a monastery and two public places, both adjacent to its cathedral, and its bishop ruled with the iron hand of a sovereign. Ideological differences came to a peak in 1371, during the 100 Years War, when Le Château supported the English and 3,000 inhabitants of La Cité were massacred.

The coat of arms of Anne Robert Jacques Turgot, governor of the province of Limousin, appeared on the first porcelain object made of Limousin clay in the early 1770s.

View of Limoges with the bridge St. Martial in foreground.

During the Middle Ages, Limoges became a stop for pilgrims on their way to the Spanish shrine of Santiago de Compostela. It was during this period that Limoges enamels became famous all over Europe. By the Renaissance, Limoges enamels and silverwork helped transformed the area into a major commercial center. During this time Limoges became known as *"La Ville Rouge"* because of the red tiles of its roofs. (During the 19th century Limoges was called *"La Ville Rouge"* because of the red glow of porcelain furnaces at night and its socialist tendencies.)

By the 17th century, the region saw numerous improvements that benefited both the citizens of Limoges and their businesses—thanks to Turgot, who served as Intendant Général du Limousin from 1761 to 1774. Originally unpopular because he called for the demolition of two of the city's most beautiful and ancient gates, he is revered today because of his fight to keep the porcelain industry within the region and for his many public works. Turgot directed the civil engineer to draw up a street plan that replaced the gates with squares, which remain today. In a town known for its fountains, he improved the water system by imposing restrictions on the disposal of waste and garbage and created restrictions for the keeping of animals. New and wider roads were built under his tutelage, making travel easier and linking the region to Paris. A royal decree issued in 1775 noted the decline of illnesses, thanks to the demolition of several ancient walls, which allowed "a freer passage of air and sunshine." Louis XVI authorized further work in Limoges, "where the population and industries are progressing." By 1791 the two rival cities were joined and

In the Right Place at the Right Time

Timeline:

1771
Limoges' first hard-paste porcelain factory established by the Grellet brothers and André Massie.

1774
La Seynie factory founded in nearby St. Yrieix.

1784
Limoges factory becomes a branch of the Manufacture Royale.

officially became Limoges. At this time the population was about 14,000.

Although hard-paste porcelain factories quickly sprang up in Paris shortly after the discovery of kaolin in France, Limoges, as a rural city, had numerous advantages over its Parisian rival. Limoges had abundant sources of firewood, taken from nearby forests and floated down the Vienne, which was needed to fire the huge porcelain kilns. It was also closer to St. Yrieix, making the transportation of kaolin easier and cheaper. Limoges also had a creative advantage: it had an abundance of skilled artisans whose skills were somewhat transferable to the new porcelain process. At the very least, the Parisian factories made for good customers—they bought their porcelain paste from the Limoges factories.

THE FIRST
FRENCH HARD-PASTE FACTORY

The development of the porcelain industry in Limoges would be directly aided by Turgot. He persuaded the Grellet brothers to become partners with André Massie, whose faïence workshop became Limoges's first porcelain factory in 1771. Work began on March 1. The first porcelain item made from Limousin clay bears the Turgot coat of arms and the inscription *"Première Porcelaine Des Terres Du Limousin"* (see page 37). In 1774 Turgot brought the factory under the protection of the Comte d'Artois, the brother of the future monarch Louis XVI, who renamed it after himself. Despite the beauty of their achievements, the partners were unable to keep the business afloat and it was acquired by the king in 1784, becoming a branch of the Manufacture Royale at Sèvres until 1796. Nevertheless, the factory continued to mark its pieces "CD"—after its original patron—until 1796.

A 1547 map of France showing Limoges in the greater Limousin area (spelled "Limofin").

In its early days, objects produced at the factory varied little—in terms of decoration and shape—from soft-paste pieces. The first pieces were white, then white and gold, or painted with little flowers. It wasn't until the workshop became a branch of Sèvres that the shapes and decoration became richer: multicolored designs of massed or mixed flowers, bouquets and garlands, along with genre paintings, pieces crosshatched in gold and masses of roses, by around 1784. In 1787, Baignol, considered the finest clay thrower at Sèvres, saw the factory through a glorious period of design.

A year later, François Alluaud took over. Despite his best efforts, the factory became run down and was sold off, passed down from owner to owner, to the present day. Alluaud died in 1799 before realizing his dream of building a large factory, complete with state-of-the-art production techniques.

Limoges has long been known for its fountains.

On the left, a porcelain fountain no longer in use at an old factory and, above,

a modern one in front of the city's train station.

*An abandoned kiln on the grounds of the former Raynaud
porcelain factory (above and left).*

*A contemporary kiln from the
Porcelaines Chastagner factory (upper right).*

*The La Seynie porcelain factory grounds
in nearby St. Yrieix, circa 1950 (right).*

LA SEYNIE (1774–1993)
LA MANUFACTURE LA REINE (1993–PRESENT)

Part of the original La Seynie factory, established 1774, which no longer stands today.

Two generations of the Marquet family, Paul Marquet
and Jean Paul Marquet, shown in the factory's French country dining room, where the elder
Monsieur Marquet serves traditional French fare (facing page).

Though La Seynie was not the first factory in Limoges (it is actually in St. Yrieix but near enough to bear the name of its neighbor) it is worth mentioning because it has survived almost three centuries.

Founded by the Comte de la Seynie (who had become wealthy by selling kaolin from his St. Yrieix property) and his two cousins, La Seynie was granted permission to produce porcelain by the French Minister Bertin, provided that it:

- bear a distinctive trademark to distinguish it from Sèvres
- be exclusively white or decorated in blue—all other colors and the use of gold were strictly prohibited.

The partners agreed to the requirements, and, although they had the money, they still lacked the technical and practical experience to run a porcelain plant. They found what they were looking for in the persons of an industrial chemist named Fournerat, formerly with La Manufacture du Comte d'Artois (the first Limoges factory) and Monsieur Baignol, of Sèvres fame, who would later go on to head the Limoges factory. Baignol took over the factory in 1789 and was followed by numerous other owners until the Marquet family assumed control in 1950. The factory was renamed "Manufacture de la Duchesse de Berry" in 1823 and later became known as Manufacture La Reine.

In 1775 one of the partners requested of Minister Bertin

that the factory not be held to his restrictions, to which the minister replied: "Should you succeed in achieving durably the standard of quality found in the royal production, the king will dispense you of observing the restrictions concerning the use of colors and gold." A year later, the general superintendent for the entire Limoges district offered his support for the partners, citing the high quality of the biscuitware and the color decorating. Moreover, the high quality of the local kaolin paste allowed La Seynie to produce a white porcelain that many considered to be on a par with Sèvres. Nevertheless, the request was still turned down. Over the years, despite the minister's ruling, it is said that some of the owners seemed to have taken delight in not observing the restrictions.

By the end of the 18th century, French porcelain had reached an age of unprecedented beauty and craftsmanship. The perfectly vitrified quality of the paste, its brilliant whiteness, and the clarity of the designs elevated porcelain-making to a new level. Technology had aided art, and porcelain craftsmen rose to the occasion by creating objects that became more and more beautiful.

A small museum featuring porcelain in one of the old factory buildings on the grounds of Manufacture La Reine.

Louis XIV, the "Sun King."

The 18th century is considered one of the most fertile periods in French history. But it would take the efforts of a 17th-century king, Louis XIV, to propel France into an era of unprecedented cultural growth, economic strength and cultural vitality.

Louis XIV came to power in 1661, when he decided to rule France alone, without a prime minister. An absolute ruler, the monarch declared in his famous statement, "I am the state."

The Sun King established himself as the lead player in a kind of "theater state" with Versailles as its stage. All of the arts revolved around the king's personal taste and reflected the power and splendor of the monarch and the state. Aiming to "classicize" culture, Louis XIV established academies of dance, science, architecture and music, which set standards of taste, and subsidized writers who contributed to one of the most fertile periods in French literary history.

Louis XIV was a great builder who paid special attention to decorating and furnishing, and since the numerous artistic institutions were under his control, they sought to achieve his ideal of somber dignity and magnificence in all respects. That ideal is no better represented than in Versailles. Louis furnished Versailles with works from the Manufacture Royale des Meubles de la Couronne at the Hôtel des Gobelins in Paris, which drew craftsmen, painters, weavers, silversmiths, metalworkers, mosaicists and embroiderers from all over the world to create luxurious furnishings for the

The Cultural Climate of France: Setting the Tone for World Taste and Design

Timeline:

1661
Louis XIV, the "Sun King," comes to power in France, beginning an era of unprecedented growth and artistic achievement.

1715–74
Reign of Louis XV, characterized by more lightness and gaiety in the arts.

1774–92
Reign of Louis XVI.

1796–97
Term "rococo" coined.

king's residences. Versailles became the epicenter of taste and refinement for the elegant and aristocratic, whose reverberations were felt all over Europe—and beyond.

Under Louis XIV France's boundaries expanded, but, as a result of numerous battles at its borders, the state sank deeper and deeper into debt. The king was forced to levy additional taxes, which would darken his legacy by the time of his death in 1715.

LOUIS, LOUIS: XV AND XVI
Louis XV, the Sun King's great-grandson, who reigned from 1715–74 and Louis XVI, who reigned from 1774–92, were unable to capture the glow of the Sun King's grandeur, but continued to make minimal improvements. While the powers of the monarchy weakened, the economy became stronger. Many of the debts incurred under Louis XIV were settled under the reign of Louis XV, the sciences flourished under a renewed sense of scientific enlightenment, and, beginning in the 1720s, France embarked on a new cycle of growth.

Artistically, the heavy dignity of the Sun King's reign was replaced by a gaiety and lightheartedness that would become the rococo, the thoroughly French version of baroque, under Louis XV and XVI. While the Sun King's legacy was reflected in a classical symmetry and order, his successors ushered in a more flirtatious feeling, which was expressed in the avoidance of straight lines, the use of light color and much gilding.

So revered was French style and influence that most German princes spoke French and tried to emulate French style. Prince Carl Eugen (1728–93) of Württemberg employed a full-time consultant in Paris whose responsibility was to supply him with all new publications, court circulars, and manuals of architectural and decorative style.

Even though the Germans had been enjoying objects made of a superior quality of porcelain for many decades, the inspiration for many of their designs during this period came from France. Engravings of paintings by French rococo artists became popular sources for painters of porcelain boxes.

Louis XV

Louis XVI

Hot-Air Ballooning

Many of the milestones of hot-air ballooning occurred in eighteenth-century France, an activity Marie Antoinette called "the sport of the Gods." In August 1783, a 13-foot-diameter balloon was filled with hydrogen gas and released near Paris. When it landed 15 miles away in the countryside, local peasantry believed it to be a monster and stabbed it with their pitchforks.

In September of that year, at the Chateau de Versailles, a 74-foot hot-air balloon was released before a crowd that included King Louis XVI and Marie Antoinette. Carrying a cockerel, a duck and a sheep in its basket, the balloon drifted for eight minutes before landing one- and- a- half miles away. The bird was pronounced fit for consumption, while Marie Antoinette became enamored with the sheep and claimed it for her private zoo. Louis XVI proposed that the first human to take to the skies should be a criminal from the Bastille, but the nobility were aghast that such a momentous event should be credited to a convict. Monsieur Jean-François Pilatre de Rozier and his friend Major François D'Arlandes volunteered for the event. On November 21, 1783, before a crowd that included the king and queen, the balloon rose 500 feet and floated over the rooftops of Paris for 25 minutes before landing safely almost six miles away, becoming the first manned balloon flight.

In the midst of all this excitement in the arts, sciences and humanities, Europe was soon to be transformed by a substance that, 300 years later, is still the object of addiction and controversy—tobacco. Discovered by Columbus, tobacco was imported to Europe by Spain. The conquistadors called it "tabac," after the name "tsibatl," given to it by the Indians of the Caribbean. Spain continued to be the major European importer of tobacco until the early 17th century, when English colonists began growing it in Virginia. Snuffing, the inhaling of powdered tobacco often combined with other aromatic ingredients, was first observed as early as 1493 by Friar Ramon Pane, who had accompanied Columbus and remained behind as a missionary. Early snuff-taking in Europe began in Spain and Portugal, and later spread to the other Roman Catholic countries— Italy and Ireland—before infiltrating the rest of the continent. It was "by the nose" that tobacco made its entrance into France.

Snuff Culture: Europe Embraces an Epidemic

Timeline:

1493
Snuff observed by Friar Ramon Pane of Columbus's expedition.

1560
Snuff introduced to French Queen Catherine de Medici.

1624
Pope Urban VIII threatens those who use snuff in church with excommunication.

1725
Snuff-taking reaches dramatic proportions; Pope Benoit XIII revokes a bill banning the use of tobacco in sacred places.

Snuff takers prepared their snuff according to personal taste. If you didn't make it yourself it could be prepared by tobacconists, who sold it. Snuff could be scented with orange blossoms, roses or an aromatic bean from the tonka tree, musk or bergamot.

One Jeanne Baptiste D'Albert de Luynes, who at 13 became the wife of the Comte de Verrue, created a number of mixtures to satisfy the noses of the rich and famous who dropped by. Among the 60 pots, urns and boxes in her home were snuffs from the East India Company, which were used by the queen, and other varieties enjoyed by the likes of Cardinal de Rohan and the Elector of Hanover.

SNUFFING FOR HEALTH

Physicians and scientists, including Nicot, originally believed that tobacco was a cure-all for everything from migraines to toothaches, bad breath, sneezing, upset stomach and the common cold. During the plague of 1614, snuff was taken in England and again during the more famous plague of

The French ambassador to the court of Portugal, Jean Nicot, introduced snuff to Catherine de Medici in 1560 as a cure for her headaches, making her the first royal snuff taker. For many years afterward snuff bore the title in France of *"Poudre à la Reine,"* and French botanists were so delighted with Nicot that they immortalized him by using his name to create the botanical term for tobacco—*Nicotiana tabacum.*

Snuff was made by grating about four pounds of pressed and cured tobacco with a snuff rasp or small grater. In its early days, snuff takers carried the rasp so they could prepare the powder as needed. Simon Barbe recommended in *Le Parfumeur Français* that only a pound of snuff be blended at once, and then kept in a tightly sealed jar or box to preserve its "virtue and smell."

1665, when it was recognized by doctors as an antidote. Before long, people began to enjoy snuff under everyday circumstances and not just when the plague threatened. As snuff-taking became more popular, the backlash against it became more pronounced.

Though many governments prohibited snuff-taking, and often tobacco smoking as well, those who snuffed continued to defy laws and medical advice—as well as other threats—to oblige their habit. Europe was soon in the grips of a nicotine habit it could not shake off.

Perhaps the most ardent opponent to snuffing was the Catholic Church, which was the first to preach of its uses and abuses. Even though the church equated snuff-taking to heathen witchcraft, it was unable to keep its own clergy, as well as its con-

In 1560, snuff was given to Catherine de Medici, Queen Mother of France, as a cure for her headaches, making her the first royal snuff taker.

You Are How You Sniff

Even the *way* snuff was taken reflected one's social breeding. The art of snuffing was taken so seriously, a guide to it was published anonymously in France about 1750 listing 14 steps to undertake what has been called a delicate "ballet of the hands."

1. Take the snuffbox in your left hand.
2. Flourish the snuffbox in your left hand.
3. Tap the box (to settle the snuff).
4. Open the snuffbox.
5. Offer the box to the company.
6. Now bring the snuffbox back toward you.
7. Keep the box open.
8. Tap the box and the side to collect the snuff together.
9. Take a pinch of snuff in your right hand.
10. Keep the snuff in your fingertips for a little while before inhaling it.
11. Bring the snuff to your nose.
12. Breathe in strongly with both nostrils and without grimacing.
13. Sneeze, cough, spit.
14. Close the snuffbox.

DUGAZON, dans SGANARELLE DU FESTIN DE PIERRE
Comedie

N.º 16.

A Paris, chez Martinet, rue du Coq, N.º 15.

Il purge, rejouit conforte le cerveau;
De toute noire humeur promptement le delivre,
Et qui vit sans tabac, n'est pas digne de vivre:

Acte 1.re Scene 1.re

gregations, from snuffing. Snuff-taking during high mass reached such proportions that in 1642 Pope Urban VIII—who had condemned Galileo—had to threaten those who snuffed in church with excommunication.

In Russia so many poor people were spending all their money on snuff that it was outlawed in 1634. Almost 10 years later, Tsar Michael proclaimed that anyone found guilty of taking snuff for a second time would have his nose amputated.

As early as 1584, the widespread use of tobacco in England caused Queen Elizabeth to prohibit it, and by 1604 James I issued a treatise warning against the harmful effects of tobacco, incorporating the Church of England's opposition to its narcotic effects. By 1625 the use of tobacco for medicinal purposes was widely discredited all over Europe.

In France Louis XIII also tried to abolish the exotic plant, allowing tobacco to be purchased only through a physician. His successor, Louis XIV, also an ardent anti-snuffer, ordered his physician to address the court on the evils of snuffing. The Sun King so detested tobacco that no one at the court dared produce a snuffbox in the royal presence. Charlotte d'Orléans, married to the brother of Louis XIV, wrote in a letter from Versailles that snuff-taking had contributed to the homeliness of her granddaughter. In it, she displayed her disappointment in not seeing what had been a beautiful girl turn into a beautiful woman: "She has developed a mania which has spoiled everything. She had the prettiest little nose, as young children have. I know what happened. She has been permitted to take snuff and this is why she has such a big nose now." Charlotte wrote later that "there is nothing more despicable and more disliked by the king, and still his children and grandchildren are doing it without any regard for the fact that the king hates it."

In a conciliatory mood, the Sun King tolerated its usage during Mass. He allowed only a single pinch to be taken by those in the royal court and only the "*marguillet*," the lay person in charge of overseeing the church, could offer the *tabatière* to the courtiers. Louis felt that the clacking of the lids, and the accompanying sneezing and snufflings, diminished the solemnity of the service.

SUCH FASHIONABLE STUFF

Nevertheless, snuff continued to be sniffed by court society at the perpetual social affair that was Versailles. Sarcastic writings of the period described the court beauties of Louis XIV with their painted cheeks and "*le nez, barbouillé de tabac.*" Even without royal approval, by the mid-17th century snuff-taking had become an extremely enjoyable social indulgence and a symbol of vanity and fashion.

By the end of the century, a dramatic change in the attitude toward snuff-taking took place. What had until this time been a habit—be it good, bad or harmless—had developed into an important social grace. Engraver Marin Engelbrecht (1684–1756) captured this transformation in the title of his brass engraving, "*Jam most est, quod medicina fruit*" ("What used to be medicine became fashion"). During a period of indulgence that swept France under Louis XV, snuff played an important part in this new age of playful elegance. *L'exercice de la tabatière* ("the exercise of the snuffbox") was so revered it was almost considered an art form. As a result, the period has been called the "*Siècle de la Tabatière.*"

In many ways snuff was the perfect pastime during this age of idle enjoyments. Courtiers, who spent hours waiting in anterooms and galleries, once passed the time entertaining themselves with silly toys and *divertimenti*. Snuff-taking became a suitable replacement for such distractions, and the snuffbox became their calling card, signaling their status and standing.

For some, instruction on the proper handling of a snuffbox, along with the correct way of conveying the coveted dust to the nostrils, required more formal education and schools were created to that end. One, in London, taught young merchants from the Royal Exchange how to offer snuff to a stranger, a friend or mistress, "with an explanation of the careless, the scornful, the politic, and the surly pinch, and the gestures proper to each of them." The same school also trained the etiquette-obsessed on the proper use of the fan. Commenting on the phenomenon, Alexander Pope (1688–1744) wrote:

Snuff or the fan supply each pause of chat
With singing, laughing, ogling and all that.

So ingrained in the society had snuff become, it inspired everything from poetry to parody. Jean-Baptiste Lully's *Ballet de l'impatience* (1661) included a 3-voice choral canzonetta of the "snuff takers." In 1664 Molière opened his play *Don Juan* lauding snuff, which he called "*la passion des honnestes gens.*" "There's nothing like tobacco," he wrote. Without it, he asked, what was the point of living? Snuff "not only cheers you up and clears your brain out, it actually teaches you how to be virtuous and…respectable.

J'AI DU BON TABAC

Songs About Snuff

The following was penned by Gabriel-Charles de l'Attaignant, born in 1697, a popular writer who entered a religious community and eventually became the ecclesiastical dignitary of Reims. He nevertheless frequented salons, cabarets, even the *tripots* (cafés with a room for gambling and cards in the back). He also wrote songs, including drinking songs. Never hesitating to turn out an epigram, L'Attaignant almost got himself badly beaten by the Count of Clermont, whom he had insulted. L'Attaignant got his revenge by refusing the count the most elementary courtesy—a pinch from his tobacco box. Here's the translation:

> To that good gentleman
> Of Clermont-Tonnerre,
> Who was unhappy
> At being included in a song,
> Threatened
> With a beating,
> One replies to him,
> And deflects the blow:

> I have good tobacco
> In my tobacco box
> I have good tobacco
> You won't get any of it.

J'ai du Bon Tabac

> I have some good tobacco
> In my tobacco box
> I have some good tobacco
> But you won't get any of it.

> I have some of excellent quality
> And ground to perfection
> But it's not for your ugly nose!

Haven't you noticed how well people behave as soon as they start taking it, how pleased they are to offer it round, wherever they are? They never wait to be asked, you see, because tobacco makes you so honourable and…virtuous that you anticipate people's wishes." And, despite the Sun King's prohibition of snuff, it nevertheless became a clandestine craze, judging by the popularity of Simon Barbe's *Le Parfumeur Français,* a recipe book for scenting snuffs, which went into four editions between 1693 and 1698.

Another social commentary comes from the English writer George Eliot (1819–1880), who observed that "…the most gluttonously indefinite minds enclose some hard grains of habit; and a man has been lax about all his own interests except the retention of his snuff-box, concerning which he was watchful, suspicious, and greedy of clutch."

Satirists had a ball with snuff—and all of its idiosyncrasies. One of the funniest descriptions of a snuff taker comes from the English satirist John Heinrich Cohausen, who in his *Lust of the Longing Nose* (1720) writes:

> Do but notice what grimaces snuff takers make, how their whole features are convulsed, how they dip into their snuffboxes in measured rhythm, cock up their noses, compose their mouths, eyes, and all their features to a pompous dignity, and, as they perform the solemn rite of snuff-taking, they look as if they scorned the whole world, or were bent on some enterprise of which they might say, like Bouflet, "I will make the whole world tremble!"

Shakespeare even got in on the act—although there is debate among historians as to whether the great bard is actually referring to snuff or some other aromatic powder. He mentions "a certain lord" "…perfumed like a milliner" holding a pouncet box "twixt his finger and thumb":

> He gave his Nose, and took't away again;
> Who there with angry, when it next came there
> Took it in snuff…"

By the second decade of the 18th century, snuff had spread through all classes of society and was being sniffed by men, women, even some children. At this point even the Church gave up trying to regulate its use: in 1725 Pope Benoit XIII revoked a bill banning the use of tobacco in sacred places. Nevertheless

many believed in restraint during ceremonies. Women took snuff with such frequency in church that one English newspaper in 1709 had to speak out against it. A period book of etiquette also advised Christians not to indulge in their habit during services:

> It is showing very little wisdom not to respect God and his Word, as shown by infrequent visits to church or no visit at all, and when one does go, in never praying to God our Father . . . in sleeping, applauding . . . knocking out chairs and benches, making eyes to women . . . and constantly having a tabatier [sic] in hands . . . . "

Even the holy fathers were dipping into the sinful box. One Italian writer observed in 1768 that old Italian friars were all taking snuff and had to be making it themselves since they were too poor to buy it.

Also during this time, snuff-taking became extremely fashionable for both gentlemen and ladies. Though women enjoyed far fewer rights than men in 17th- and 18th-century France, they were permitted to partake in *l'exercice de la tabatière*. Imagine these elegant ladies, in their elaborate gowns of satins and lace, indulging in a habit that could cause some distasteful results. To solve the problem, some snuffboxes came equipped with mirrors so the user could wipe away any unsavory remains that settled around the nostrils. The English writer and politician Sir Richard Steele (1672–1729) poked fun at the problem this new habit posed for women during mealtime: "an upper lip mixed with snuff and the sauce . . . for everyone to observe."

Among the elite, snuff itself was as sacred as one's pipe. When someone took a pinch from George II's snuffbox, which was lying on a table, he threw it out the window. Frederick the Great was a bit kinder. Upon discovering a page purloining a pinch from his box, he exclaimed, "Boy, put that box in your pocket; it is not large enough for the both of us."

THE CULT OF THE TABATIÈRES

As snuff-taking achieved cult-like popularity all over Europe, the snuffbox took on greater importance. At the height of its popularity the snuffbox became as revered as the habit itself. The mere appearance of this tiny object revealed the position, taste and wealth of its owner. Just like fans, canes and swords, a beautiful *tabatière* was meant to be flourished and made part of one's elegant attire and persona. The shell, which became a decorative symbol of the 18th century, reflecting the rhythm, elegance and fantasy of the times became a popular subject for porcelain snuffboxes.

Originally, snuffboxes with mirrors were used to help snuffers wipe away any tell-tale traces. Contemporary versions (left) make a beautiful addition to any dressing table.

Another important symbol of the ancien régime was the pug, the favored lapdog that was synonymous with aristocratic society. Because of the pug's unflagging popularity, savvy box makers created snuffboxes in their images, either in paint or molded porcelain.

Snuffboxes were so much a requirement of luxurious attire, even those who didn't snuff were advised to carry one nevertheless, according to a 1783 book of etiquette. Portrait painters during this period often included a snuffbox in their paintings as a symbol of elegance and fashion.

summer box light. And this refinement has been so exaggerated that boxes are changed every day and it is by this distinguishing feature that one recognizes the man of taste."

Appropriately, being such a treasured item, snuffboxes became the perfect gift for life's most important occasions in the 18th century. In addition to those used for political purposes (see *Boîtes à Portrait* and Gold Boxes, page 70), snuffboxes were the traditional coming-of-age gift from father to son and could be used as a legacy left by a dead friend. As a gift to thecastrato Farinelli, the Prince of Wales in 1735 presented him with jeweled snuffboxes.

By the middle of the 18th century there were snuffboxes for everyday use and those for elegant occasions. Accordingly, the richness of the boxes had to correspond with that of the rest of the costume and environment. Some dandies changed boxes daily, or according to their mood. The truly stylish would have as many snuffboxes as outfits. A 1782 issue of the *Tableau de Paris* reported, "One has boxes for every season. The winter box is heavy and the

Indeed, by the end of the 18th century, it became clear that snuff—as well as the container it was held in—had created a culture uniquely its own. If there were one image to characterize the entirety of rococo society, it would be that of a gentleman of fashion delicately pinching snuff between thumb and forefinger from an elegant *tabatière*.

The pug was the coveted lapdog of the ancien régime and one of its most important symbols. This Saint-Cloud box (above) dates from 1750–55.

Portrait painters often included a snuffbox as a symbol of elegance and fashion. In this portrait, Maria Luisa of Parma (1751–1819) is holding a tabatière à cage containing a miniature painting presumed to be of her husband.

That snuff should end up in a box is more the result of need than of fashion. After all, most boxes are merely covered containers which start out being utilitarian but end up being much more. Boxes reveal to us the pleasures and pastimes of a culture, by storing not only commonly used items but that which is precious and meant to be preserved or set apart from the rest. Boxes have stored money for safekeeping, contained secrets scribbled on paper and held love notes and military commands that have changed history. Whether they held bibles, as some early American boxes did, or an infant's lock of hair, boxes often changed hands many times. The best of these functional objects, which portray an elegance in design or craftsmanship, are meant to be displayed and treasured. Even though their original use may have become obsolete, beautiful boxes have continued to retain their appeal over the centuries as valuable objets d'art.

A History of the Tabatière

TIMELINE:

1325 B.C.
King Tutankhamun of Egypt is buried—along with a great assortment of the earliest boxes.

4 B.C.
Ceramic arts in ancient Greece flourish. Boxes are among those ceramics.

100–500 A.D.
Romans create a number of new boxes and forms to fill practical needs.

1681
First snuffbox introduced.

1728
Circular, oblong and double boxes first appear.

1735
François Boucher, a court artist who influenced all the arts, including snuffbox-making, creates his first royal commission—four paintings at Versailles.

1740–50
Shoe snuffbox is produced at Chantilly.

1806
Napoleon orders 100 *boîte à portrait* boxes made for his supporters.

Some 18th-century snuffboxes were a bit larger than most. This hunter at left (St. Cloud, circa 1740) which Rochard has reproduced (right), is a good example.

The earliest boxes date to ancient Egypt, a civilization known for its share of indulgences. In those days, a person was buried along with his or her belongings and boxes were created to hold everything from food to perfumes. Not surprisingly, it was the tomb of King Tutankhamun (r. 1334–1325 B.C.) that yielded the greatest bounty of Egyptian boxes, revealing the remarkable craftsmanship of early artisans and those things that were important to this society. The ancient Egyptians loved their toiletries—especially cosmetics—and its games. It was during ancient Egypt that boxes for toiletries—by far the largest category of boxes throughout the ages—first appeared. Surely it was a finely crafted cosmetics box that Cleopatra used to apply powder and paint. Egyptians played games similar to chess and checkers and created small boxes for them. Materials ranged from the simplest, in wood or woven reed, to solid gold, carved alabaster or precious

woods such as ebony and cedar inlaid with ivory or lapis lazuli and encrusted with semiprecious stones.

In classical Greece, when ceramic arts in the Aegean flourished, earthenware boxes were often painted with figures using one or two earth tones, in addition to black. Either round, square or rectangular, these boxes were used for cosmetics, unguents, perfumes and food. Box-making would undergo a new surge of creativity under the more pragmatic Romans, who developed a number of new uses for boxes. In addition to carved ivory or alabaster boxes called *pyxides* that held toiletries and salves, Romans created large storage chests and trunks to hold clothing and all sorts of wares. Many new forms including boxes with flat, domed or peaked tops began to appear.

With the introduction of Christianity, ornamentation on boxes began to change. Images of Pan and Bacchus were gradually replaced by those of Father, Son and Holy Spirit. The end of the classical period, however, did not signal the end of its influence. From the Renaissance right down to the 18th century, European decorative artists continued to be influenced by Greek and Roman style. And snuffboxes were no exception.

THE FIRST SNUFFBOXES

The earliest snuffbox dates back to 1681, the same year the word "snuffbox" was first used. The name *tabatière*, or snuffbox, originated in France in the middle of the 17th century and refers only to those boxes used for snuff. Kandler, the master designer of the

Meissen factory, first preferred the term "*boîtes à tabac (à priser)*," or snuff tobacco box, early on in his career, but later referred to *tabatières,* a trendier name.

From the mid-17th to the mid-19th- centuries, snuffboxes were manufactured all over Europe, especially in France, Germany and England. Few were made in Spain or Italy, even though the custom was popular there. America had virtually no snuffbox production; they were imported from Europe.

Though snuffboxes were produced for over 200 years, the art of the snuffbox reached its highest form in the 18th century.

SIZES AND SHAPES

Snuffboxes existed in all shapes and sizes, from very tiny to large. The earliest examples were at most about 2.5 inches large, but later boxes were bigger, stretching what some consider to be the definition of snuffboxes to more than three inches long.

Unlike other miniature boxes, snuffboxes were at once public and private. They were meant to appear on one's dressing table or carried in the pocket, but they were also shared with others in public and designed to intrigue.

Fashionable snuffers wanted more than anything to possess a box that was different from everyone else's and would, when produced, create a sensation. This caused much competition among boxmakers to create a box that was novel, without being ridiculous, in an attempt to please their wealthy and discriminating patrons. The makers of snuffboxes seemed to be at no loss for creative

The nun (at left) was made at St. Cloud, circa 1740, while the box on the right is Rochard's contemporary version.

ideas—a myriad of shapes and themes were produced in every imaginable material.

Book-shaped boxes made their debut in 1710. By 1723, circular, oblong and double boxes had first appeared. A box in the shape of a sedan chair was introduced between 1727 and 1732.

Round and oval boxes were popular during the 1740s and 50s, followed by a penchant for deep, oblong *à cage* boxes, created by having gold frames hold porcelain or ceramic plates, during the 1760s and 70s. These enameled gold boxes were painted with landscapes, scenes from village life, hunting scenes and the great *châteaux* of France, the most popular of all.

The discoveries at Pompeii and Herculaneum began a classical revival, using forms and motifs discovered from the sites. Shell or cartouche-shaped boxes were in vogue during the first quarter of the 18th century, followed by the oval box during the second half of the century. Oval

boxes often included a central motif surrounded by a decorative border, usually of enamel work.

There was a shape for every interest and every passion, from the macabre—coffins or skulls as a *memento mori* of a dead friend—to the novel, including Napoleonic hats and helmets, fish heads, human heads, goldfinches and pugs. Coquilla nuts were carved into human heads, tortoises, boars' heads, dogs' heads, pigs, fishes and more.

MATERIALS AND DESIGN

Snuffboxes were made from materials that ranged from the everyday to the highly prized and exotic to accommodate snuff-takers of modest and more affluent means. Wood, lacquer, papier-mâché and enamel were used, along with materials more costly and difficult to work, including tortoise shell, bone and horn. Straw-work snuffboxes were made in France beginning about 1750. To commemorate one's trip, a souvenir box might have

Boxes took every conceivable shape. Above, an English box, circa 1760, in the form of a young girl's masked face, was adapted into a modern version (left).

Antique shoe-shaped boxes such as this one made at Chantilly (left) were variously used as snuffboxes, vinaigrettes, nutmeg graters, matchbox holders or signets. The Rochard version appears at right.

been crafted in rock salt, coal polished to look like black marble. Eighteenth-century visitors to Vesuvius might return with a snuffbox made from lava. Wooden-shoe snuffboxes, considered the epitome of the cobbler's craft, were often created to mark graduation from apprenticeship.

Boxes made of gold, silver or enamel were often encrusted with pearls or diamonds. Chinoiserie designs decorated with tinted shells and mother-of-pearl, and tortoise shell boxes adorned with piquè work and panels from the studios of painters of miniatures were also popular.

THE APPEAL OF THE MINIATURE

The fact that snuffboxes were miniature—a necessity of course if they were to be held in a pocket or the fold of a belt—gave them added preciousness. In terms of technical prowess alone, a miniature demanded more skill from all involved in its creation. In fact, miniature representations of everyday objects were attractive to most craftsmen. The miniature shoe, for example, while a popular snuffbox design, was also used as a vinaigrette (an ancient method of perfuming), nutmeg grater, matchbox container and signet.

A snuffbox had added appeal because its use was not strictly utilitarian, but rather an indulgence, albeit a small one. Toylike, with dimensions of dollhouse proportions, a tiny box has always had irresistible appeal to every age and sex. Opening one requires a slow and delicate hand. Such careful movements lengthen the suspense and heighten the drama of opening a box, only to discover a portrait, miniature landscape, flower, initials, a mirror or some other surprise under the lid. Sometimes a flower was conveniently used to disguise an imperfection.

This tiny armoire and chair are testimony to the enduring appeal that miniatures have always had with boxmakers (left).

Oval boxes, such as this modern version made by Rochard (top right), were first introduced in the second half of the 18th century.

The surprise beneath the lid of this chinoisserie-style box (1723–24) from Meissen is a spray of flowers.

Baroque vs. Rococo

The 18th century has left us with two very influential styles that continue to be collected and copied today: baroque and rococo.

Baroque: Broadly defined, it refers to a style that flourished in the 17th and early 18th centuries. The hallmark of the style is the dramatic emotional intensity that it evokes—it addresses the senses directly. Baroque art often uses vigorous movement to draw the eye to the center of the work, sharp contrasts between light and dark, relief or stuccowork, and opulent fabrics. According to the *Dictionary of Art* (Macmillan Publishers Limited, 1996) it "addresses the senses directly through emotion rather than reaching the intellect through reason."

Rococo: Coined in 1796–97, the term "rococo" was named after the French word *rocaille*, meaning the rockwork or shellwork that was found frequently in rococo decoration. Essentially French, this style developed under the reign of Louis XV and spread throughout Europe. Characterized by lightness, grace and playfulness, rococo was a reaction to the heavy, formal atmosphere favored by Louis XIV. Soft colors and delicate curves, the use of gilding and mirrors to create a sparkling effect, and dainty decorations, usually garlands and flowers, produce the playful gaiety and elegance of the style.

Double boxes, such as this 1750—60 Meissen box (left), made their debut in 1723 and are still being made today(right).

From every blush that kindles in thy cheeks,

Ten thousand little loves and graces spring,

To revel in the roses.

—NICHOLAS ROWE (1674–1718)

Boîtes à Portrait

Boîtes à portrait, or portrait boxes, were often gold boxes that contained portraits of the king, or other aristocratic figures, and later, Napoleon. They were given by royalty as a mark of their favor, and a visible token of royal esteem, a custom that lasted in France from 1688 until Napoleon's time. They were also used to commemorate certain royal occasions. Royalty also gave portrait boxes as family mementos. Many princes or dukes, especially those who were the patrons of a porcelain factory, had boxes commissioned in their likenesses.

Boîtes à portrait were given as presents in most courts of Europe; one observer noted that after William Pitt's resignation it "rained snuffboxes" to commemorate the event, but in no other country were they as lavish or given quite as frequently as in France.

Early examples were often of dark tortoise shell, lined with gold, in round, oval or rectangular shapes. The portrait was enamel and usually on the cover. In 1662, Pitan, Louis XIV's jeweler, created a more elaborate style of box and at his death in 1676 his successor, Pierre de Montarsy, continued to devise new patterns for the *boîtes à portrait,* which, because of the king's dislike of snuff-taking, were never called snuffboxes or *tabatières.*

Under Louis XIV these small boxes were intended to hold a lock of a lady's hair or an appropriate poem. They could

Types of Snuffboxes

Napoleon was one of history's great snuffbox collectors and the subject of many portrait boxes.

also be used, in keeping with the cloak-and-dagger antics at Versailles, as message carriers to be sent to one's mistress or lover. Ultimately, however, their real purpose was often to deceive the king. During the long reign of Louis XVI, an age rich with gift-giving—carpets, swords, jewels, gold—his image appears perhaps more frequently than any other monarch on *boîtes à portrait.*

In 1806 Napoleon had about 100 gold portrait boxes made as tokens of appreciation for his closest political supporters. Indeed, some believed that politics and snuff-taking went hand in hand. The French statesman Talleyrand declared that the use of snuff was an essential of diplomacy, "for a man had time enough to compose his features and collect his thoughts while he opened his box and extracted a pinch."

Gold Boxes

The Sun King's abhorrence of snuff-taking discouraged the production of gold snuffboxes, as did the Sumptuary Edict of 1700, which was designed to conserve the nation's gold reserves because France had become bankrupt again. But neither was totally effective in preventing *l'exercice de la tabatière.* Boxmakers found ways to bypass the law, devising the *à cage* style, which used a minuscule amount of gold.

But the prohibition only ended up defeating itself. The rich simply went

Within the Lid the Painter plays

his Part,

And with his Pencil proves his

matchless Art:

There drawn to Life some Spark or

Mistress dwells,

Like Hermits chast and constant

in their Cells.

…were a strict Inquiry to be made

Through all the Town, and ev'ry

Box survey'd

You'd seldom find the Picture of

one Spouse.

—Pandora's Box, a Satyr Against Snuff
(London, 1718)

abroad to buy their snuffboxes, causing a rise in imports and a defeat of the edict. Finally, the Regency of 1721 permitted that the gold used for snuffboxes be increased to 7 ounces and native production was encouraged to compete with imports. Of those gold boxes that were made despite the law, not one has survived.

PORCELAIN SNUFFBOXES

Some historians believe that jeweler Lazare Duvaux (see page 76) was the first to have launched the porcelain snuffbox craze; many were described in his famous diary.

The simplest were rectangular, round or oval, ranging from 3 to 10 centimeters (1 to 4 inches).

Snuffers bought their porcelain boxes directly from the factories or from factory stores. Or, if you had substantial resources, you could custom-order a box from a jeweler who could create the metal setting and make the box to your specifications.

DECORATION

The decoration on 18th-century porcelain boxes incorporates in miniature the most popular decorative themes of the period. Early examples are of chinoiserie scenes or ornamentation inspired by Kakiemon decoration. Others are painted with popular hunting scenes, real and imaginary landscapes, soft floral bouquets, scenes of dwarfs, peasants, and mythological figures and allegorical scenes. During the height of a craze for flowers of all kinds, especially tulips, a popular enamel box developed, containing floral patterns over a white or black ground.

Unlike snuffboxes made of gold, silver or other materials, the design of porcelain snuffboxes often featured the most beautiful designs on the inside lid, where it would be revealed as a wonderful surprise when the snuff was offered. Often many of the decorations inside bore no relation to those on the outside of the box.

THE ART
AND THE ARTIST

The relationship between fine art and the fine art of porcelain was symbiotic. In fact, many of the arts of the time were called upon to help fashion an 18th-century box. On a small scale, the box represents the greatest technological achievements of all the decorative arts. The art of the sculptor and carver are represented, along with architectural detailing and techniques found in fine furniture and

François Boucher (1703–1770), Artist to the King and the World

A painter, tapestry designer, set designer, etcher and draughtsman, Boucher is considered to be the most influential artist—of both fine and decorative art—of the 18th century. A number of his designs were copied in miniature by porcelain painters to decorate snuffboxes. And his models for sculptures of children became porcelain figures at Vincennes and Sèvres.

Stylistically, Boucher has been called "a dispenser of sweetness," credited with reinventing the pastoral, a romanticized scene that depicted shepherds and shepherdesses as sentimental lovers, and for his nudes, nymphs and cherubs in idealized

mythologies. Two of his most celebrated compositions are *Diana After the Bath* (1742), now at the Louvre, and the *Triumph of Venus* (1740).

Boucher's first royal commission came in 1735, when he painted four large pictures at Versailles. By mid-century he had delved into tapestry design—in those days a tapestry was an essential part of a fashionable home—and had become the favorite court painter for Louis XV and his mistress, the Marquise de Pompadour. Boucher taught her how to etch and she encouraged Boucher to create frivolous mythologies and pictures of children mimicking adult activities, as well as a number of portraits of herself.

cabinetmaking. The finishing touch was in the hands of the painter, whose work required more skill to be created in miniature.

The work of many fine artists of the time influenced the designs and miniature painting that appeared on porcelains. Indeed, at Sèvres, porcelain was meant to compete with painting. Most of the porcelain painters remained anonymous, but they often directly copied the style of well-known painters, and sometimes—in these days before copyright laws existed—a particular painting or etching. One of the most frequently copied painters of the age was François Boucher (1703–1770), the court artist to Louis XV (see facing page). Aptly described as "a dispenser of sweetness," his idealized pastorals, girls, women, nymphs and nudes—what we would today consider the epitome of rococo—were copied from Saxony to Sweden.

At Sèvres, many artists of the court were encouraged to apply their skills to this new medium, among them the goldsmith Duplessis, the enameler Mathieu and the chemist Jean Hellot. The sculptor Étienne-Maurice Falconet was appointed to the factory in 1757. His work, very influenced by Boucher, was usually of nymphs. The quality of his workmanship, his innovative techniques and his use of color gained him notoriety in France.

METAL SETTINGS

Joining the two pieces of porcelain together with mountings made of silver, gold or brass required the skill of a jeweler or smith. In fact, the metal setting is the one thing all snuffboxes have in common, regardless of shape. Porcelain snuffboxes were either mounted at the factory

This lamb was among the small animal snuffboxes that Saint-Cloud produced in the second quarter of the 18th century.

by smiths or sold as porcelain pieces to jewelers in Paris, who created the mountings themselves. Many of the boxes that were sold to jewelers were usually larger and meant to be displayed in boudoirs or on drawing room tables. Often, the settings proved more fragile than the porcelain; hence, our many old snuffboxes with modern hinges.

Gold- and silversmiths also figure into the history of porcelain snuffboxes in another way. Having appeared in gold and silver, as well as other materials, before they appeared in porcelain, many of the early snuffbox shapes were taken from the work of these craftsmen.

Saint-Cloud was the first of the French factories to produce porcelain snuffboxes, beginning about 1731 and continuing for the next 20 years. Many were in the baroque style. A 1731 advertisement for the Paris branch of the factory described *"Tabatières de toutes sortes de contours, garnies & non garnies."* ("Snuffboxes of many shapes, decorated or not"). These would have been shell-shaped or circular boxes, rather small, painted, sometimes on a colored ground, with boldly outlined Chinese figures and landscapes.

Around 1725 boxes with raised gilded decoration painted over with translucent colors appeared. During the second quarter of the 18th century, Saint-Cloud began producing interesting small snuffboxes in the form of sheep and other animals, mounted in silver or gold. The figures were always in a supine position so that the object could slide easily into a pocket. Although the factory operated until 1766, snuffboxes do not appear to have been made after 1750.

Chantilly is perhaps most famous for the creation of the high-heeled shoe, around 1740–50, most of which were decorated with florals. (see page 65). The form appears slightly later in Mennecy, where, from about 1750, numerous snuffboxes were made. Oblong shapes dominated the 1750s, followed by a decade of ovals. Typical Mennecy boxes are molded all over with a basketweave or waffle pattern, with flower sprays on a white background. This basic decoration, in addition to occurring on the usual oval and oblong examples, is also found on boxes in the shape of miniature commodes, hearts, baskets, or trunk-shaped boxes.

Vincennes-Sèvres has left us with few examples of snuffboxes, perhaps because most of these were sold as luxurious objects, set in gold and often encrusted with diamonds for an exclusive clientele. As a result, Sèvres boxes are extremely rare.

A Rochard basket-shaped box adorned with a heart cutout.

Jeweler to the Royal and Rich: Lazare Duvaux (1703–58)

Fortunately for the collectors of snuffboxes, history has left us with the business diary of Lazare Duvaux, a Parisian goldsmith to the king and a *marchand-mercier* who supplied the courts of Paris and Versailles with luxury items of all kinds, from lacquer furniture from the Far East to porcelain snuffboxes. Duvaux's diary provides us with many fascinating details about his clientele and their spending habits.

Like many of the shop owners and jewelers of the Saint-Honoré and Place Dauphine neighborhoods of Paris, Duvaux was always trying to keep alive the interest of his clients. Porcelain provided jewelers with another small luxury item which they could improve upon and make their own. In fact, Duvaux, a shrewd businessman, is credited with being "the first

to measure the advantage of the use of porcelain to achieve the decoration of these boxes." That is, he used porcelain plates from Sèvres and mounted them "*à cage.*" Duvaux also embellished boxes in precious jewels.

In addition to providing us with insight into the types of snuffboxes that were custom-made for royalty, the diary also sheds light on just how clever a businessman Duvaux was. A case in point: how he handled a frequent customer of his, a certain Marquise de Pompadour. Duvaux wrote of delivering to her an oval snuffbox from Sèvres, which cost 600 pounds, and charging an additional 760 pounds for gold hinging. If you consider that he charged the Duke of Villeroy 144 pounds for a pair of candlesticks "gilded with ormolu," it could be said that, in the case of the marquise, royalty had its price.

Other Uses of Miniature Boxes

If they didn't hold snuff, miniature boxes held sweetmeats (a candy often made from sugared fruit), patches, perfume or small jewels. Many of these boxes were often indistinguishable from each other. Small boxes were also used as nutmeg graters, or to hold toothpicks or soap. Some were made into little vinaigrettes (called the pomander or pouncet box during Elizabethan times), which continued to be used well into the 18th century. These boxes contained a tiny sponge soaked in aromatic vinegars seasoned with combinations of nutmeg, cloves, cinnamon, wormwood, camphor, rose-water, lemon juice and other aromatic ingredients. Believed to guard against infections, these concoctions also served as primitive deodorants in an age when showers and baths were few and far between. Henry VII carried a pouncet box of gold or silver encrusted with jewels. He and his courtiers hung their pouncet boxes from their waists by a cord or had them set into their walking sticks.

Intended also for display as decorative works of art, beautiful boxes were made for virtually no purpose at all. As objets d'art, they were used as gifts and as special containers of treasured objects.

In 1891 one could find bonbons, bite-sized chocolate candies, or sweetmeats in this delicate bonbonnière made of Limoges porcelain.

her boudoir. The ritual began with a foundation, a plaster made of white clay, honey and gum or the more dangerous ingredients of powdered pearls or white lead. Rouge, commonly made from cinnabar, or red mercuric sulfide, a poisonous substance that was known to cause ladies to lose their teeth, was then applied. Another type of rouge made from cochineal, or carmine, was safer but pricier. Upon visiting the exclusive rouge maker to Queen Marie Antoinette, the Baroness Oberkirch noted:

The smallest [rouge] pot costs a Louis, and for one above the ordinary one must pay 60 to 80 Louis. She [Mademoiselle Martin] has permission for rouge pots to be made specifically for her at Sèvres. These she sends to Queens, a Duchess can barely obtain one by chance.

The finishing touch was the application of patches or *mouches*, beauty spots made of gummed taffeta in the shape of moles, stars or half-moons. They were strategically placed near the lips, eyes, décolletage or some other suggestive location, allowing one's lover to know one's availability or state of mind. Patches were also enlisted to hide unsightly blemishes, including scars left after the smallpox epidemic.

Few women of fashion emerged from this elaborate ceremony before noon.

PATCH BOXES/ROUGE POTS/POWDER BOXES

The beauties of the 18th-century court were known for using their feminine charms—no matter how obvious or artificial—to lure and entrap. To assist them, various containers were needed to dispense their maquillage. Often, but not always, these boxes would have detachable lids, since they were meant to be prominently displayed on a dressing table and not carried about. Some, with attached lids, contained mirrors for a quick touch-up later in the evening.

Putting on one's face was an elaborate, possibly dangerous and often quite public beauty ritual that could take place while the lady's admirers, hairdresser, musicians, tradesmen or religious advisors paraded through

BONBONNIÈRES/SWEETMEATS

Deliciously decadent bonbons, bite-sized chocolate candies, became the delicacy of choice and those who indulged could not be without them. Men as well as women carried these *bonbonnières*, or *"drageoirs"* as they were then called, in their pockets. Legend has it that François de Lorraine, Duc de Guise, was in the act of eating a bonbon when he was assassinated by a man named Poltrot. Even stranger, his son, surnamed Le Balafré, was enjoying the same delicious treat when he was

Each piece in the Rochard chess set is meticulously crafted as an individual box.

*Contemporary Rochard designs such as the camera and fish boxes
are popular with modern collectors.*

murdered in the Château de Blois, by the Guards of Henri III in 1588. *Bonbonnières* were also used to hold sweetmeats to *se fortifier l'estomac* (fortify one's stomach) between meals. The diary of Lazare Duvaux finds Madame Pompadour ordering one sweetmeat box in French porcelain, adorned with pictures of children and decorated with gold.

THE STUFF OF FOLKLORE

Snuffboxes had so captured the hearts and imaginations of those all over Europe, they naturally became colorful subjects for folklore. Because they were small and easily hidden, snuffboxes also became involved in a number of intrigues—from affairs of the heart to affairs of the state.

As a Political Symbol. When Napoleon was banished to Elba and the Bonapartists were plotting for his return, they filled their boxes with snuff scented with violets, his favorite flower. In order to determine where a person's sympathies lay, a pinch of snuff would be offered, along with the loaded question: "Do you like this perfume?"

As a Lifesaver. The Comte de Guiche, madly in love with the daughter of Charles I, "La Belle Henriette," wore her portrait in a gold snuffbox suspended from his neck. During a battle, the snuffbox deflected a bullet that would have likely killed him. Of course, it was the great love he had for Henriette—and not the snuffbox—that he credited for his salvation.

As a Means of Identification. In a terribly confusing tale called "The Ghost of Count Walkenried," which appeared in an 1823 English book called *Ghost Stories*, a gold snuffbox is used by a banker to identify the son of a friend before advancing him some money for travel. The snuffbox contains a portrait of the elder count—to whom his son bears a striking resemblance—and had been given to the elder count as a gift from the banker. The young Count Walkenried dies, however, before the banker is able to meet him, but his "ghost" appears, leaving the banker with the gold snuffbox and some jewels. After the ghost's exit, the banker checks the portrait and notices that indeed the ghost did bear a resemblance to the count's father. In the end it is revealed that the ghost was in fact a friend of the young count, a Baron von Vigny, who looked so like the count they often dressed up as one another. It seems the moral of the story is: even if a snuffbox contains an accurate portrait, it is no protection against wicked practical jokers.

The Pug:
A Box for the Collectors'
Favorite Dog

The pug—a breed that is enjoying cult-like popularity and whose image has become a favorite among collectors—was not only the favorite dog of the 18th century, but, like the snuffbox, also one of its most important symbols. It was a pug that bit Napoleon as he crawled into bed on his wedding night and a pug that carried messages to a jailed Josephine. And of course it was a pug that curled up on the lap of Madame Pompadour, the king's mistress who, through her influence, would become one of the century's great arbiters of taste.

Originating in China, where they were revered for the way the folds on their brows seemed to form the character for prince, pugs became pets of the middle class in England during the rein of Queen Victoria. And collecting pug paraphernalia has never waned since that time. Some well-known aficionados were the Duke and Duchess of Windsor, whose collection included a pug pillow and candle-holders, which were auctioned at Sotheby's in New York in 1998.

Pugs adorned the lids of snuffboxes and were painted on enamel boxes, made in France and England during the 18th century, that were used to hold perfume or candies. At the 1998 Winter Antiques Show in New York, a four-inch candy box with a pug on the lid sold for $9,800. According to the *New York Times*, pugs today are most collectible as ceramics, porcelain in particular. A pair of Meissen porcelain pugs was recently valued at $18,000.

The Art of Collecting

"Collecting is a world habit. Collectors practice it consciously and with a definite, recognized aim. The rest of us practice it more or less unconsciously."

—Arnold Bennett (1861–1931)

The influential Marquise de Pompadour, a mistress to Louis XV, was an ardent supporter of the porcelain industry and was said to have had a snuffbox for every day of the year.

In today's market, 18th-century boxes are such coveted antiques that they fetch quite a bit of money at the world's great auction houses. "They're absolutely charming," said Christie's Jody Wilkie, vice president and head of European ceramics and glass. Passionate collectors travel the world and spend thousands for just one addition to their collection. At a 1997 auction of European ceramics held at Christie's in London, a Saint-Cloud silver-mounted snuffbox, circa 1748, modeled in the shape of a sheep, sold for $3,450.

Early collectors were no less enthused about their tiny possessions. As miniature symbols of power and prestige, snuffboxes became objects of obsessive collecting. Here are some of history's most famous — and infamous — enthusiasts:

Marquise de Pompadour
(1721–1764)

Known more commonly as Madame de Pompadour, she was born Jeanne-Antoinette Poisson to a middle-class family. She received an excellent education and was introduced to high society by a wealthy businessman. When she met the king at a ball in 1746 she left her husband and moved to Versailles to become one of Louis XV's mistresses, as well as his political advisor and private secretary. She exerted her will, her influence and her taste in the court and at Sèvres. As an ardent supporter of the Royal Manufactory, she placed frequent special orders for porcelain snuffboxes and is rumored to have had one for every day of the year. She was honored by some porcelain makers, who used her spaniel as an image for a snuffbox, and ridiculed by others. A Mennecy box, in the form of a lady reclining on military equipment, is believed to be a satirical depiction of the power-hungry marquise. Nevertheless, her influence on all of the arts during this time cannot be disputed.

Here is a sampling of some of the porcelain boxes Madame de Pompadour ordered from Sèvres, according to the diary of Lazare Duvaux.

• *December 1751:* sweetmeat box painted with children and garnished in gold.
• *December 1757:* a sweetmeat box, garnished in gold.
• *January 1758:* a gold-mounted sweetmeat box with green mosaic, painted inside with a miniature.
• *October 1758:* oval snuffbox painted with animals, garnished with colored gold and lines.
• *November 1758:* square snuffbox, "very well decorated" with animals and garnished with a double gold mount of colored gold.

Napoleon Bonaparte
(1768–1821)

An inveterate snuffer and collector of snuffboxes, the Emperor of France (1804–14) is also rumored to having had one for every day of the year.

Because he suffered from occasional bouts of choking, Napoleon also carried a *bonbonnière* at all times and used the chocolates to quell his cough. Count Corti, in *The History of Smoking* (1931), commented that "If one could collect all of Napoleon's snuffboxes in one room and arrange them in chronological order, they would form a picture history of his life."

COUNT HEINRICH VON BRUHL (1700–1763).

As the prime minister of Saxony, he oversaw government and the administration of the Meissen porcelain factory from 1733–56. One of the perks of being its director was permission to help himself to stock and have special orders made free of charge. Indulging in his passion for snuffboxes, he was reported to have had a collection of 700 boxes, many of which were gold and bejeweled. He also possessed:

"at least 300 Suits of clothes… A painting of each suit, with the particular cane and snuff-box belonging to it, was very accurately drawn in a large book, which was presented to his Excellency every morning by his Valet de Chambre, that he might fix upon the dress in which he wished to appear for the day."

Rochard's double-hinged box isn't used by pranksters as the early versions were.

Envelope boxes, similar to this one (right) with an elaborately painted note inside, were in vogue during the reign of Catherine the Great.

Among her favorites, which were bought in a Parisian antiques shop:
• a puzzle box with a double lid so the owner could secretly admire a picture of his mistress without raising his wife's suspicions.
• a joker's snuffbox made with double hinges that created two compartments. After the owner took a pinch of snuff, it would be turned over and an empty box offered to the unsuspecting friend.

PHILIPPE D'ORLÉANS (1674–1723)

Upon the death of Louis XIV, the Parisian parliament installed the Sun King's enemy, the Duke of Orléans, as regent for Louis XV from 1715–23. An ardent snuffer himself and an admirer of beautiful objects, he greatly encouraged the snuffbox makers. Despite the fact that France was virtually bankrupt, he fulfilled his passion for snuffbox collecting without restraint. Legend has it, he, too, had a box for every day of the year.

Known as a demanding taskmaster, von Bruhl ordered a white relief porcelain box particularly difficult to make. Kandler, the master modeler at Meissen, describes it in May 1737:

Begun one very toilsome snuff *tabatière* for His Excellency Privy Councillor von Bruhl on which there are many flat decorations and there are also to be extracts of hunting scenes on the lid and sides, and which, however, has to be completely finished in the next month.

MADEMOISELLE COLETTE D'ARVILLE

A soprano of the Opéra Comique in Paris during the 1930s, she loved collecting 18th-century snuffboxes, *bonbonnières*, patch boxes and powder boxes as much as she liked to sing. She was quoted as saying: "A snuffbox is like a thoroughbred animal. An authentic pedigree increases its value, especially if it can be connected with a famous historical figure."

FREDERICK THE GREAT (1712–1786)

This Prussian king who ruled from 1740–86 ordered large numbers of porcelain snuffboxes to satisfy his passion for collecting. At the end of the Seven Years War the king became personally interested in the Meissen factory, where, in 1765, no less than 11 varieties of snuffboxes were produced.

CATHERINE THE GREAT (1729–1796)

Born a German princess, she ruled as empress of Russia from 1762 until her death. Her collection of snuffboxes was most likely international. Russian boxes tended to reflect the styles set at Meissen. During her reign "envelope" boxes, often with French inscriptions, were in vogue. The bottoms of boxes were often imprinted with the family's coat of arms.

Closely associated with rococo society, the cult of the *tabatières* would eventually disappear along with the ancien régime. Rumblings of the revolution appeared in various forms, none more bizarre than the snuffbox, which began to fall out of favor as a symbol of luxury and coveted object of the elite. Even as the aristocracy faded, the snuffbox continued to reflect societal changes. To display one's displeasure with the king and queen, snuffboxes were covered with fish skin, called *shaguen*, similar in pronunciation to the word for grief in French, *chagrin*. Miniature portraits of the royal couple were then placed in the lid, surrounded by "*La Consolation dans le chagrin.*"

After the taking of the Bastille, snuffboxes were mounted with pieces of stone from this despised jail. Patriotic slogans, the entire lyrics of a revolutionary anthem—even the likeness of the guillotine—were used to adorn snuffboxes, not made of gold or porcelain, of course, but the more pedestrian materials of wood, horn or tortoiseshell.

After the revolution, as the rich sought to relinquish any semblance of luxury in a desperate barter for their lives, snuffboxes became among the many precious items that were exchanged—for the rags of a peasant, for example, or a carriage for escape. Snuffboxes would survive the revolution, but in a form that was more utili-

The End of an Era

TIMELINE:

1789
Bastille stormed in Paris. Start of the French Revolution.

1792
Louis XVI is overthrown.
First Republic established.

1804
Napoleon crowned emperor.

1815
Napoleon's defeat at Waterloo.

tarian than aristocratic. Like the pug, another symbol of the leisure class, snuffboxes became an object of ridicule during the bourgeois period. By the turn of the century they were used more often as souvenirs than as holders for snuff.

Perhaps a more symbolic ending to the era of the snuffbox came on the evening of June 18, 1815, with the capture of Napoleon's carriage at the Battle of Waterloo. Napoleon had escaped, but his possessions were inventoried by a Prussian officer. Among them "Napoleon's own diamond snuffbox," which was documented in remarkable detail. It was:

a most magnificent and beautiful article, in the finest taste and exquisite workmanship; it is of a lengthened form and made to be held in and opened by one hand; it is of fine gold, enameled; the lid of dead gold, with a border of brilliance of the finest water, set in the form of bees. The center is enriched by his initials, in fine diamonds; the whole number of which, on the lid, are one hundred and forty-four.

Napoleon would reign no more and the snuffbox would move from the palms and pockets of the ruling classes into private collections and the world's great museums, where they have remained for posterity, for all to admire.

A
DESCRIPTION
OF THE
COSTLY AND CURIOUS MILITARY CARRIAGE
OF THE LATE
EMPEROR OF FRANCE,
TAKEN ON THE EVENING OF THE
BATTLE OF WATERLOO;
WITH ITS
SUPERB AND CURIOUS CONTENTS,
As Purchased by Government,
AND NOW EXHIBITING (BY PERMISSION) AT THE
LONDON MUSEUM, PICCADILLY;
WITH THE
CIRCUMSTANCES OF THE CAPTURE,
ACCURATELY DESCRIBED, BY
MAJOR BARON VON KELLER,
BY WHOM IT WAS TAKEN AND BROUGHT TO ENGLAND.

LONDON:
PRINTED FOR THE PROPRIETOR,
WILLIAM BULLOCK;
AND SOLD AT THE PLACE OF EXHIBITION,
LONDON MUSEUM, PICCADILLY.
1816.

A diamond snuffbox was among the items found in Napoleon's carriage captured at the Battle of Waterloo.

THE CAPTURE OF THE MILITARY CARRIAGE
OF BONAPARTE,
TAKEN ON THE NIGHT OF THE BATTLE OF WATERLOO;
and now exhibiting by permission of Government
at the
London Museum Piccadilly

He leaped out & jumped upon his Horse without his Sword, losing his Hat which fell off
(vide Bluchers Letter,)

London Published as the Act directs 1st Jany 1816, by W. Bullock London Museum Piccadilly

PART THREE

*Limoges Becomes a
World Leader in Porcelain
Production*

The Golden Age

*Limoges:
A Sense of Place*

Limoges Becomes a World Leader in Porcelain Production

With Napoleon exiled to the British island of St. Helena after his defeat at Waterloo, power in France shifted back to the Bourbons, in the person of Louis XVI's brother, Louis XVIII, and to a rising bourgeoisie made up of the professional classes, the bureaucracy and the peasants who were freed of their serfdom and given the possibility of a better life. This new social landscape had a profound impact on the economy of France. In Limoges, the Restoration first brought optimism and then prosperity to the porcelain industry.

During the first half of the 19th century, the cost of Parisian manufacturing rose, making porcelain, already a high-stakes, high-profit venture, even riskier. Just as the glassmakers of the Middle Ages moved from Venice to Murano, so, too, did the porcelain manufacturers move from Paris to Limoges. The Limousin countryside provided firewood for kilns, and the skilled and unskilled laborers who worked for wages below those of Paris. The Vienne River was used to transport wood to the kilns and to power the mills that ground kaolin into paste.

Porcelain factory buildings were built around the all important kiln, as seen in the above print.

PORCELAIN SHOWS PROMISE

In 1801 the hard-paste factory in Limoges that had been a branch of the Manufacture Royale was taken over by the son of its former director, also named François Alluaud. About the same time Étienne Baignol, who had also worked at the factory and had been a co-worker of the elder Alluaud, moved his own small factory from St. Yrieix to the former site of the Petit Augustins convent in Limoges. Both men are considered to be founders of the Limoges china industry. According to Limoges expert John Merriman, these two factories soon accounted for three quarters of the porcelain produced in Limoges at the time.

By 1816 Alluaud realized his father's dream: he moved his factory from the Rue des Anglais to a new, state-of-the-art facility in the sparsely populated Faubourg des Casseaux, near the Vienne, becoming the first building in Limoges that was created specifically as a porcelain factory. Alluaud became the most important porcelain manufacturer in the city at this time, employing 150 workers. His artistic efforts were recognized in 1819, when he received a silver medal for his porcelain at an important exposition in Paris.

The same year Alluaud opened his new factory there were four other porcelain factories in operation in Limoges; by 1825 there were eight. By 1830 there were 9 factories, accounting for 14 kilns. But despite its rapid growth, porcelain manufacturing in Limoges was still overshadowed by the textile industry.

Limoges

TIMELINE:

1815
Napoleon exiled to the British island of St. Helena in the South Atlantic Ocean. Bourbon dynasty reestablished in the person of Louis XVIII.

1816
François Alluaud, after taking over his father's porcelain business, builds a state-of-the art factory that becomes the first building in Limoges created specifically as a porcelain factory.

1819–25
Factories established on the outskirts of the city.

1841
American David Haviland arrives in Limoges and shortly thereafter begins exporting porcelain to the U.S.

1847
Haviland sets up a decorating workshop. By the 1860s Haviland becomes the largest producer of porcelain in France.

1872
Number of workers in porcelain industry equals half of all the region's workers.

1850–1925
The "Golden Age" of Limoges porcelain industry.

INTO THE COUNTRYSIDE

Though Limoges proved a less expensive place to produce porcelain, some entrepreneurs realized that they could reduce costs even further by moving farther into the countryside. Between 1819 and 1825, factories were established in Magnac Bourg, Coussac Bonneval, Solignac, St. Brice and St. Léonard. These locations were even closer to the kaolin mines and provided better access to firewood and cheaper labor. At the same time, the German, Spanish and Italian markets began to open up, paving the way for French imports. Despite an economic slump in 1826–27 and a rise in the price of wood, the entire region was soon prospering from porcelain. The number of people employed by the porcelain industry grew from 200 in 1807 to over 1,800 in 1830.

FROM LABORER TO ARTISAN

Larger companies especially required great numbers of workers. During the height of the 19th-century market, the major factories employed about 1,000 laborers. Sometimes entire families worked for companies; many were women and children. By 1855 Alluaud's factory, in the Faubourg des Casseaux, employed 224 men, 51 women and 30 children, in addition to the gilders and porcelain painters, who were considered artists and, therefore, separate and distinct from the factory workers.

Porcelain manufacturing required a wide range of expertise, from low-paid rural laborers to highly skilled artisans, decorators, turners and molders who came from other cities. The school of industrial design that the Société d'Agriculture et des Arts established in 1804 also provided the factories with trained workers.

The Vienne River was used to transport firewood
from the countryside to the kilns.

By mid-century porcelain manufacturers were encouraging the training of local skilled decorators to replace those trained in Paris or Sèvres. To further encourage the industry, the government began subsidizing classes in molding and casting, drawing and mathematics.

Generally speaking, the level of skill increased the farther along one went in the production process. Manual laborers called *flotteurs de bois* lifted the wood from ramps on the sides of the river and hauled it to the factories. Low-paid, unskilled workers from the countryside extracted kaolin from the quarries and transported it to small *moulins à pâte,* where the paste was readied for production, shaped into balls and delivered by wagon to the factories. There the paste was beaten and kneaded to remove any air bubbles before given

to turners, who shaped the pâte on a pottery wheel with a knife. Molders removed further residues and shaped each piece, usually with a mold. The pieces were then fired in huge kilns, stoked by men called *hommes du four,* and dipped into enamel (feldspar and powdered quartz diluted with water). Workers dubbed *engazetiers* placed the porcelain in clay vessels that protected it from cinders and ashes. Oven workmen called *enfourneurs* oversaw the final baking, which took between 30 and 45 hours at very high temperatures. When finished, the *useurs de grains* checked for imperfections, while burnishers and polishers completed the process.

At that point, the *artistes en porcelaine* took over. They applied the ornamentation, using the tiniest brushes. Once they had put their creative stamp on a piece, the porcelain was briefly reheated

*The upper levels of this building were left open
so air could circulate and dry the kaolin.*

in *moufles,* or smaller ovens. At this point the porcelain was complete and ready for shipment.

Porcelain artists made up a highly paid and relatively independent group, especially for those times. Most worked at home. As Merriman explains, they were dignified, literate, prosperous and as close to an "aristocracy of labor" as existed in Limoges. Many of these artists had arrived from Sèvres, Paris or other towns where their skills were in demand, before coming to Limoges during the Restoration. Some transferred their talents to other artistic endeavors. Auguste Renoir, for example, who was born in Limoges, began his career as a porcelain plate painter before becoming famous for his fine art.

TWO TYPES OF OWNERS

Overseeing the entire process were the owners (and by the mid-18th century factories would be designed so they would literally be able to do so). According to Limousin historian Alain Corbin, they were likely to be one of two types: either a descendant of the 18th-century manufacturers, who were considered to be a part of the bourgeoisie, or an entrepreneur who probably had experience in the industry and had pooled his resources to create a small factory. These paternal overseers frequently labored beside their workers and became much beloved figures. Often the children of the entrepreneurs would learn the trade of their fathers and eventually take over the business.

This pulley system dates back to the 19th century when it was used to haul kaolin up from the mines (left).
Raw kaolin is still found scattered throughout this abandoned mine in St. Yrieix (right).

Alluaud and Baignol were considered the latter type of patron. During the depression of 1826–27, Alluaud's workers agreed to a 20 percent reduction in salary so that the business could survive. Baignol was so well loved by his employees that they fought with his survivors over the right to carry him to his grave.

François Pouyat was also in this category. A porcelain artist and manufacturer of the ancien régime known for his whiteware, he had been involved in a number of small factories in St. Yrieix and Paris and at one time had been partners with Baignol. By the 19th century, his sons, Emile, Leonard and Charles-Louis, continued his work in a small factory on the Place des Carmes.

Alluaud and Pouyat had additional advantages. Both had been landowners in the St. Yrieix vicinity, so they not only mined the kaolin, but made the porcelain paste, which was sold all over Europe. By the time they opened factories, they had already become successful businessmen.

THE HAVILAND INFLUENCE

David Haviland was an owner who didn't fit in either category. As an American, he was among a group of outsiders who would make inroads in the Limoges porcelain industry, though few would have as important a role in the development of Limoges as a porcelain center of international acclaim. Already part of the American bourgeoisie, Haviland hailed from a New York family of importers and, with his brothers, was a partner in Haviland Brothers & Co. Originally, the brothers specialized in English faïence, but an economic crisis in 1836 made business difficult. Intrigued by French porcelain, David thought it might have a place in the American market.

At the time Haviland and his wife arrived in Limoges, there were 11 porcelain factories operating in and around the city. He began hand-picking porcelain from selected factories and shipping it to New York. By 1847 he had created a decorating studio

A Limoges Folk Art:
Porcelain Cemetery Plaques

Not surprisingly, manufacturers of Limoges porcelain have continuously sought new uses for the product that has given their region so much notoriety and wealth. One of these products, porcelain cemetery plaques, became an industry in the Haute-Vienne region.

Originally made in the shape of a porcelain dinner plate, plaques were either embedded in a headstone or freestanding. Some were made into free-form shapes. Hand-painting by artisans then decorated the plaques, reflecting the unique characteristics of the deceased. Flowers, biblical and religious tableaux,

joined hands and portraits of death were some of the themes employed. Today examples of such plaques can be seen in cemeteries throughout the region.

The high point of this folk art was between 1850 and 1870, during the so-called Golden Age of Limoges porcelain production. Today only a few plaque painters remain. Manufacturing processes have also changed, making the plaques more resistant to the forces of nature so they can, according to an epitaph on a funerary plaque, "perpetuate throughout the ages the memory of the Limousin people."

Whiteware: Decorating for Each Market

Before the arrival of David Haviland, a shortage of *artistes en porcelaine* had forced most companies, with the exception of Alluaud, to ship their porcelain to Paris for decoration. As a result, by 1850 much of the Limoges production was in undecorated porcelain, primarily tableware, called whiteware or blanks. Pieces that were not shipped to Paris were exported to the U.S. to be decorated there by commercial workshops or by individuals. China-painting had become such a popular American pastime, special schools were established to teach the skill to enthusiasts.

This arrangement proved lucrative for the Limoges industry, which no longer faced the competitive threat of Parisian factories. The Parisian porcelain manufacturing industry had so dwindled that by 1850, only 17 porcelain factories were listed in the Paris directory, while 75 porcelain decorating firms were listed. At the same time, having focused on producing whiteware made it harder for Limoges to establish an artistic reputation for itself. It would take several international competitions, the continuing Haviland influence, and a receptive American clientele—among other factors—before Limoges porcelain would make its decorative mark on the world.

Whiteware is still produced in Limoges, either to remain unadorned or to be decorated at an artist's workshop (above).

Whiteware from La Reine, circa 1950 (right).

in Limoges where porcelain was painted in a style that he thought would please his American customers. The business was an immediate success—so successful in fact that some even consider the opening of Haviland's workshop as the "true beginning" of the modern porcelain industry in Limoges, creating yet another debate in the history of porcelain. Opinions aside, what is true is that porcelain finally became the number one industry during the middle of the 19th century, due in part to the success of the Haviland clan but also due to the failure of the textile industry, which was unable to keep up with competition from the north.

In the United States, it seemed everyone, including President Lincoln himself, wanted Haviland china. Haviland responded by creating a presidential set, the first of many that would grace State dinners at the White House for years to come. A gift of Haviland china was considered a status symbol for new brides, but even the housewife was not overlooked, as she could purchase a set through mass retailers such as Macy's. A 1910 catalogue from that store offered a 101-piece "Real Limoges French China" set for $17.99.

Haviland distinguished itself from other porcelain companies in Limoges by specializing in dinner services—in thousands of patterns—and by focusing entirely on the American market. Typically, a Haviland set was decorated with transfer decoration or hand-painted with delicate floral patterns, in a simpler style more preferable to American taste. Other companies in Limoges also produced dinner services, not as well designed but much more lavishly decorated.

While Americans preferred a more restrained style of dinnerware, their taste in objets d'art was a bit more ornate. After 1850, many workshops specialized in selling to Americans decorative pieces that were more traditionally French, with a richer palette, depicting scenic, floral, fruit or figural themes that made heavy use of gilding. Such objects were perfect for the elaborate Victorian lifestyle.

Although Haviland originally created a workshop to paint whiteware or blanks, he believed it more profitable to control production entirely—from design to decoration—and built a fac-

tory on the newly laid Avenue du Crucifix. By the mid-1860s Haviland had become the largest single producer of porcelain in all of France. Under his influence, the use of the transfer or decal process began to spread, one of many innovations that the company would introduce. Some historians consider this development to be the beginning of the modern porcelain industry in Limoges, since the impact of the new Haviland factory had far-reaching influences on how other factories in Limoges actually operated.

When the U.S. Civil War broke out, Haviland's porcelain production almost came to a standstill, since many of its customers lived in the American South. Construction stopped and the importing business, Haviland Brothers & Co., closed down. The Limoges factory, which had been a subsidiary of the company, became Haviland & Co.

After the war, David brought his two sons, Charles, 25, and Theodore, 23, into the business. Charles quickly took over and began expanding the business by building new kilns. Within 5 years Charles Haviland turned one decoration workshop into the largest porcelain factory in Limoges.

Charles, however, was a notoriously controlling partner, which he admitted in a description of himself: "among my shortcomings the greatest may be my despotic tendencies, with a frame of mind which prevents my accepting opposition, contradiction or even argument."

Due to a family dispute, Haviland & Co. closed down on December 31, 1891, and the brothers parted ways. The following day, however, a company under the same name was reopened by Charles and his eldest son, Georges. Together they would build another factory at the Mas Louvier, and their Haviland & Co. would go on to produce a number of prestige sets for kings and heads of state. Georges would eventually close the business in 1931.

After the split, Theodore commenced building his own workshop, named after himself, on the Place des Tabacs, now Place David Haviland, and prospered. By 1906 his factory boasted 16 kilns and 800 employees. After Theodore's death his eldest son, William, took over in 1919.

The two long-competing family firms would be reunited in the 1940s, creating Haviland S.A.

The Golden Age

Though historians may argue whether the beginning of the modern porcelain industry began with the arrival of Theodore Haviland, or with the creation of the company's first full-scale factory, this much is clear: the Havilands' influence on the industry was profound. In 1905 the two Haviland brothers were employing 3,150 workers combined—representing one third of all porcelain workers. As a result of their rapid success, the Havilands focused most of the Limoges industry on the lucrative American market. According to U.S. Customs records, between 1842 and 1853 imports of French china grew from 753 to 8,594 loads. By the end of the 1850s about half of Limoges porcelain was exported to the U.S. As a result, the period from the middle of the 19th century to the first quarter of the 1900s is considered the "Golden Age" of Limoges porcelain. During this time, new manufacturing methods were introduced and the number of companies

The city of Limoges

By the middle of the 19th century, coal replaced wood as the means of firing kilns (right).

multiplied, from 32 in the mid-1800s to 48 in the 1920s, making porcelain the chief employer of the region.

In addition to the arrival of David Haviland, other developments would increase the growth and efficiency of the porcelain trade by mid-century. The most important was the replacement of wood by coal to fire the kilns at a time when the cost of wood had risen dramatically. In 1861, 16 of 40 kilns were using coal to fire porcelain. Fortunately, the arrival of the railroad came about the same time as coal, in 1856, linking Limoges to Paris, providing a faster, more direct route to decorators' workshops and foreign ports. The railroad so reduced the cost of raw materials that factories that had opened outside the city limits, though they provided cheaper labor, were now inconvenient to this new mode of transportation. The rural factories became too expensive to operate and closed down.

By the beginning of the Second Empire (1852), new markets were being found in Great Britain, Germany, Central Europe and even the Far East and South America as France began exploring new territories and trade possibilities.

Porcelain not only shaped the economy of Limoges during these years, it determined the city's development. Factories opened up in four regions of the city: from the Faubourg des Casseaux to the Boulevard St. Maurice and the Avenue of the Bénédictins; in the vicinity of the road leading to Paris; along the suburbs Montmailler and Montjovis; and from the Place des Carmes to the old route of Aixe and around the road to Angoulëme. Shops sprang up to meet the needs of the workers.

The Golden Age brought recognition for companies such as Alluaud, Haviland and others, at expositions that increased the notoriety of Limoges porcelain. In 1855 and 1867, Limoges was awarded prizes at important exhibitions in Paris and New York, respectively. At the inauguration of the Exposition Universelle in 1889, when the Eiffel Tower was inaugurated, Limoges porcelain was classified as being "out of competition" because of its beauty. Pouyat china became famous for its whiteness and translucency (the "Blancs de Pouyat") while Tharaud garnered a reputation for its tasteful decal decorations. Raud was feted for its cobalt blue *"grand feu"* coloring. It was during this prosperous time that other porcelain companies, which are still in operation today, were founded. While the Havilands were busy furnishing Americans with china, the czar of Russia ate on plates from Raynaud & Cie., founded in 1856. L. Bernardaud et Cie., created in 1863, became famous for the translucent quality of its wares. By 1890 Limoges was known as the world capital of porcelain.

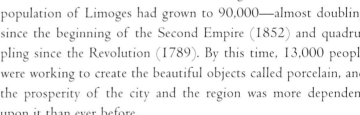

The explosion of the porcelain industry during this era happened to coincide with the Industrial Revolution in France, when assembly-line manufacturing and new inventions promised to make work and life easier. The factory was seen as man's greatest accomplishment and procedures were always closely examined to see if they could be made more efficient. One machine replaced an ancient manufacturing technique that required so-called "paste walkers" to stamp on the porcelain paste with their feet to make it more flexible. Plate-molding also became mechanized, while companies like Haviland introduced new techniques such as the imprinting of decorations by "chromolithography." The introduction of electricity in 1894 also lowered costs and made for more streamlined operations.

Nineteen-hundred was a banner year, with porcelain exports reaching staggering proportions. Production reached 3,000 firings for the 35 existing factories, and exports to the U.S. numbered 18,000 barrels. Of the 116 kilns, only 6 were still being fired with wood. The population of Limoges had grown to 90,000—almost doubling since the beginning of the Second Empire (1852) and quadrupling since the Revolution (1789). By this time, 13,000 people were working to create the beautiful objects called porcelain, and the prosperity of the city and the region was more dependent upon it than ever before.

SURVIVING TROUBLES

The Golden Age of porcelain manufacturing would be unsettled by a number of historic events, both at home and abroad. Between 1833 and 1905 worker uprisings made Limoges a hotbed of leftist activity and helped earn it the nickname "The Red City." In 1879, the average life expectancy of a porcelain

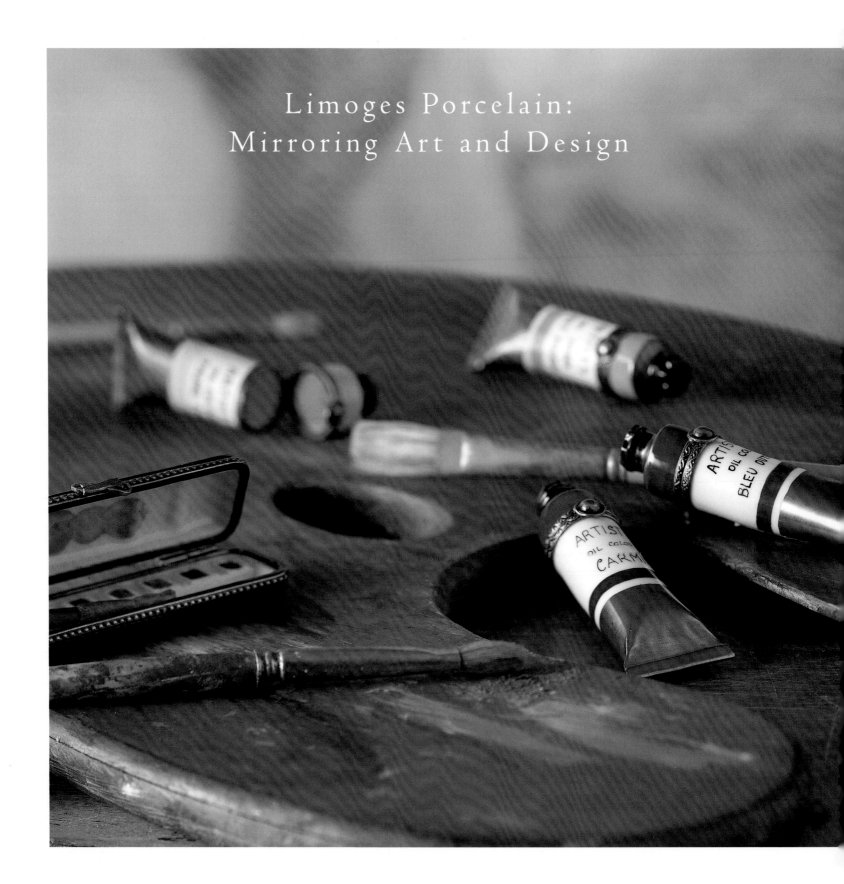

Limoges Porcelain:
Mirroring Art and Design

From the very beginning, the relationship between fine art and fine porcelain has been symbiotic. Not only did many artists get their start in the porcelain workshops in and around Limoges, some continued to work in the industry to finance their fine art endeavors. In fact, some fine artists are responsible for influencing—either directly or indirectly—the major design movements in the porcelain industry.

In the 1830s, two sculptors—Valin and Aaron—were responsible for redirecting the porcelain market from tableware to elaborately decorated gilt objects. In 1872 Charles Haviland popularized the works of the burgeoning Impressionist movement by enlisting Félix Bracquemond, an etcher and former head of the painters' workshops at Sèvres, to head Haviland's experimental Auteuil Studio in Paris. It was through Bracquemond that such artists as Jules Dalou were able to apply their artistry to the porcelain medium.

The Art Nouveau period happened to coincide with the height of the Golden Age of the Limoges porcelain industry (mid-19th century to the first quarter of the 20th century). During these years, the G.D.A. factory, under the direction of Edouard Colonna and Georges De Feure, began using underglaze decors and curved lines, mostly using green as the dominant color, with rose, light blue and pinky beige accents. The artist Samuel Bing had his Art Nouveau designs produced at G.D.A. during this period.

The Art Deco movement, virtually eliminating the frills of earlier decades, saw the likes of Jean Dufy, Camille Tharaud, and Suzanne Lalique creating sleek new motifs for tableware. The surrealist Salvador Dali made Limoges porcelain pieces, as did Jean Lurcat. For Haviland, the Swiss sculptor Edouard Sandoz created a collection of whimsical animals from 1915–20; a Wassily Kandinsky limited edition was created from a 1922 design and a 1961 Jean Cocteau drawing was turned into a hand-painted plate.

Through the years, no matter what has been popular in other decorative arts, flowers have been the most enduring type of decoration on Limoges accessories and objects, followed by gold trim.

worker was only 43 years for a man and 38 years for a woman, due in part to the danger of working with lead, used to make glazes. Sanitary conditions were short of satisfactory. There was dust from the clay, chemical fumes, suffocating heat from the kilns and 14-hour workdays. Porcelain workers were particularly susceptible to tuberculosis and other lung diseases.

In addition, new machinery replaced what was once done by hand, threatening to eliminate a number of jobs. Among those advances were new "inverted flame" kilns and the introduction of decals. Many small workshops were forced to close.

A workers' dispute in 1905 was aimed at two notorious foremen in the Haviland factories and at Theodore Haviland himself. During the unrest, prison doors were opened and the prisoners fired upon by troops; one person died and four were wounded. The redeeming outcome of these and previous uprisings is that they did result in better conditions for workers and led to the creation of the first trade union of porcelain workers, "The Initiative," in 1870.

War also affected the industry. Both World Wars virtually shut down porcelain production as men were drafted and access to raw materials became difficult. The firings at Theodore Haviland, which were up to 205 in 1914, dropped to 41 in 1917. By 1939 only 24 porcelain factories remained (in 1900 there were 34) in Limoges, employing 3,000 workers.

A heavy reliance on the American marketplace also caused many fluctuations in the Limoges economy (by 1890 the U.S. was buying half the city's porcelain production). In 1929 the stock market collapse in New York almost destroyed the industry. After hitting a low point in 1944, it took more than 30 years to recover.

A RETURN TO PROSPERITY

While every industry faces the threat of failure many times over, the Limoges porcelain industry has proved to be especially viable, bouncing back after many decades of decline. After the Second World War, more modern, efficient and less expensive methods of production, which didn't sacrifice quality and artistry, were developed. The discovery of a huge natural gas bed in the nearby Pyrenees in 1951 lead to the creation of new kinds of "cell" or "tunnel" kilns. Meanwhile, the invention of what has become a household necessity—the dishwasher—led to the perfection of chromolithography during the 1960s, with companies such as Coquet, Jammet and Seignolles being innovators. Today's pioneers are working to ensure that porcelain tableware is safe for microwave use. The 20th century has also seen the development of new porcelain markets in the fields of printing, electricity, dentistry and medicine.

In 1993 the French porcelain industry had a total revenue of over 1 billion francs ($166 million), representing 15 percent of the total yield of the French ceramics industry. The Limoges porcelain industry, comprised of about 40 manufacturers and 2,200 workers, still produces more than half of the French porcelain industry output. The majority of Limoges porcelain companies are medium-sized, small enough to maintain a high level of artistic quality while being large enough to keep up with the huge demand for their product.

The Golden Age earned the city of Limoges a worldwide reputation, but it is through the continued commitment to the creation of fine porcelain products that its legacy has endured.

"Anything stamped 'Limoges' is assumed to be of higher quality," says Eric Silver, head of 19th- and 20th-century decorative arts at the William Doyle Galleries in New York, which has featured 19th-century Limoges porcelain dinner services and decorative pieces at its auctions. "They're nicely made and have pretty floral decorations and gilded highlights. People certainly find it interesting." Mr. Silver says Limoges remains a recognizable name. "They've been developing their reputation for centuries."

Indeed, almost everywhere in the world the word "Limoges" has become synonymous with porcelain—porcelain that has a whiteness of body, an elegance in shape and design. Today, age-old companies whose wares adorn the tables of presidents and royalty co-exist with newcomers striving for the new and unusual.

For as long as needlework has been a treasured art, there have been beautiful boxes designed to hold its tools. Today, porcelain needle and thimble boxes—a favorite among collectors—can be used for their original purpose or to hold a wealth of other cherished objects.

Limoges:
A Sense of Place

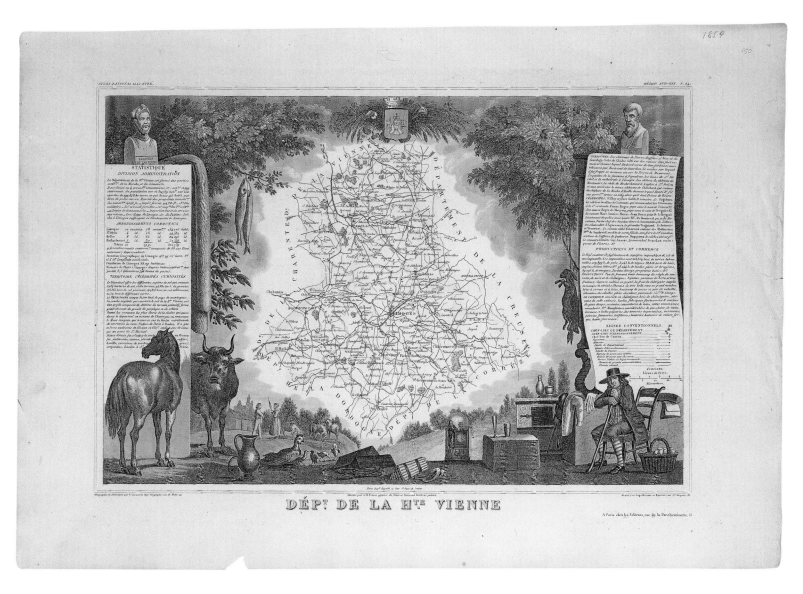

A late afternoon view of la Chapelle Saint-Aurelien near
la Rue de la Boucherie (left).

LIMOGES TRAVELOGUE: AN INTRODUCTION TO THE CITY

Getting a feel for a city begins with a map and some useful bits of information to help establish a sense of place.

THE REGION: The city of Limoges is one of 13 communities within the Haute-Vienne department, which is part of the larger Limousin province, the sixth-largest forested region of France.

HEROES AND VILLAINS: Saint Martial introduced Christiaity to the region in the 13th century. Limoges was officially united with the kingdom of France by Henry IV. "The Black Prince," a.k.a. the son of England's Edward III, burnt and plundered the city in 1370.

Facade details of the Limoges train station.

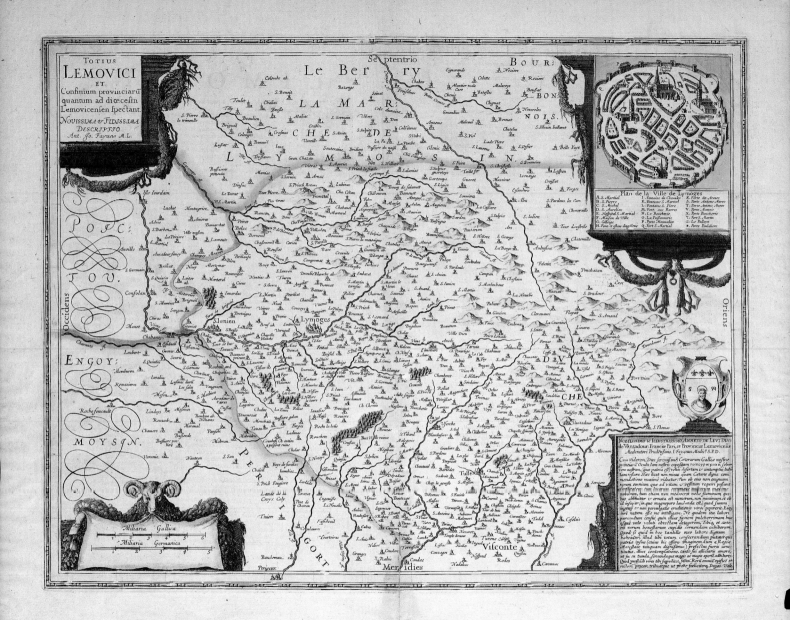

A map of the Limousin area, circa 1650.

L'Hotel de Ville, the Limoges town hall.

FOLKTALES: There is perhaps no better way to discover the character of a people than through their folktales. Those from the Limousin tend to be blunt and to the point, conveyed dramatically in very short sentences.

THE LOOK OF LIMOGES: Limoges is part of the Haute-Vienne, known as a land of grass, which when combined with the gently rolling hills creates the perfect pastureland for sheep and cattle. In fact, the Haute-Vienne has become one of the two most important regions for sheep breeding in all of France. Charming medieval houses and numerous ponds can also be seen; the Haute-Vienne boasts more than 1,751 ponds, most larger than two and a half acres.

SIGHTS: The Cathedral of Saint-Etienne was begun in the 13th century and completed in 1327. With its Roman and Gothic architecture, it contains 14th-century tombs and 15th-century stained-glass windows. The Saint-Michel-des-Lions Church, built from the 14th to 16th centuries, houses relics of Saint-Martial, as well as beautiful stained-glass windows from the 15th century. Other historic attractions include the Episcopal Palace, built in the 18th century; the Saint-Pierre-du-Queyroix Church, constructed from the 12th–16th centuries; and the Saint-Etienne and Saint-Martial Bridges, dating from the 13th century.

BIG (AND SMALL) BUSINESS: Principal industries, in addition to porcelain and enamel arts, include cattle- and sheep-raising, leather-making, tanning, electrical products, foundries, textiles, chocolates, candies and brick manufacturing.

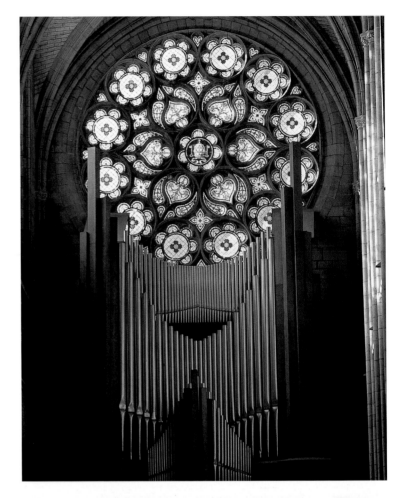

The Cathedral of Saint-Etienne.

The river Vienne

Exterior and interior views (left) of the Adrien Dubouché Museum.

FOR THE LOVER OF PORCELAIN:
THE ADRIEN DUBOUCHÉ MUSEUM

Created in 1845 by the Prefect Morisot, whose daughter was the famous painter Berthe Morisot, the Adrien Dubouché Museum in Limoges is known around the world for its fine collection of glass and ceramics, and, specifically, for its porcelain.

Adrien Dubouché, a successful businessman who was managing director of the Bisquit-Dubouché cognac company in Jarnac, was named museum director in 1865.

"Dubouché was born in the Limousin and remained very attached to the area," says Chantal Meslin-Perrier, who has been curator of the museum since 1988. "Erudite and worldly, he dedicated all of his free time and part of his personal wealth to expanding the museum's collection."

Dubouché himself donated over 4,000 ceramic pieces, glass and enamels, among which are two prestigious collections: the Albert Jacquemart, which Dubouché bequeathed in 1875; and the Paul Gasnault, donated in 1881. To thank Dubouché, the munic-

ipality asked the Council of State that the museum be renamed in his honor.

"Dubouché's enthusiasm and his lively personality allowed him to befriend many in the world of ceramics," Madame Meslin-Perrier explains. "These personal assets led to numerous gifts to the museum." The museum so grew in notoriety, the government deemed it important enough to take it over in 1881.

Today, the museum houses 12,000 ceramic and glass objects. At the center of the collection is the most beautiful and comprehensive collection of Limoges porcelain in the world. Other notable collections within the museum are its Chinese ceramics from the Tang period (19th century); European faïence of the 17th and 18th centuries; and European soft-paste porcelain (*porcelaines tendres*).

"Adrien Dubouché was a modern man who assembled a contemporary collection, which became one of the most important French ceramic treasuries of the 19th century," adds Madame Meslin-Perrier. "We are deeply indebted to him for the legacy he has left us."

Also notable is the museum's collection of 400 glass pieces from the 16th to 20th centuries, reminders of the importance of the "*arts du feu*" or "arts of the fire" tradition in Limoges.

Cour du Temple in the center of town with a view of the Consulate (above left).

Place de la Cité (bottom left).

The Cathedral of Saint-Etienne (right).

LIMOUSIN PRODUCTS AND HANDICRAFTS

With its lush forests, rolling fields and abundant natural resources, the Limousin region has given birth to unique specialty products and handicrafts that make the most of what the region has to offer.

• WINE CASKS: The proximity of dense oak forests has made the Limousin, especially its Corrèze region, well known for quality wine casks. To the viticulturist, the quality of the cask is just as important as the quality of the grapes. Different types of wood are suited to create different types of spirits. Oak from the Limousin is best suited for liqueurs.

• LEATHER GOODS: Lands ideal for grazing cattle have helped to make Limoges renowned for its leather goods.

The Weston company, a luxury-shoe maker, was created when Edouard Blanchard took over the Châtenet manufacturing plants founded in 1885. Weston is one of the companies that made Limoges famous as an important shoe-making city at the beginning of the 20th century. No less than four weeks and 200 production steps are necessary to produce one finished line. Today the company continues to sell its luxurious products through its own boutiques in Paris, Geneva and New York.

Les Chaussons Merlet, founded in 1974, specializes in shoes of a different type—those for ballerinas. In 1991 the company began creating other types of dance shoes. Each year tens of thousands of its products are shipped all over Europe.

In the center of a lamb- and goat-raising region, Saint-Junien, which is part of the Haute-Vienne, began to specialize in making leather and fur gloves and mittens as early as the 11th century. By 1655 there were 25 glove manufacturers in Saint-Junien. By the 18th century, some manufacturers took advantage of the exceptional water quality of the nearby Vienne to set up tanning and leather-dressing operations on its banks. As a result, Saint-Junien became known as the "City of the Glove," a distinction it still holds today as that industry remains the city's largest.

• BASKETS AND FEULLARD: Vast forests of chestnut trees have made basket-making an important industry in the region. To cre-

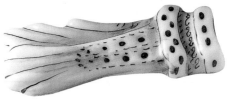

ate a perfect basket, artisans must rely on patience, precision—and the moon. Legend has it that wood cut during the old moon is easier to work.

During the 19th century, the hamlet of Mas-Gauthier, near Limoges, earned a reputation for creating chestnut boxes and baskets that were used as containers to ship all kinds of products, from porcelain to produce, all over Europe. When woven, chestnut stalks are made into attractive outdoor benches, a Haute-Vienne handicraft greatly admired by the Danes and Finns.

Today, basket-making is a small industry, employing about 2 dozen workers in 6 plants, but one that nevertheless survives due to a renewed interest in crafts.

Another by-product of the chestnut tree is the *feuillard*, a small strip of wood retaining the bark on one face or surface. These strips were used to build barrels in which food products were shipped. *Feuillard* has also been used to create casks for Irish whiskey.

• CERAMIC ROOFS: Since Roman times, pottery has been used as a roofing material in this region of France, creating a unique style. During the 18th and 19th centuries roof apexes were built to resemble ears of corn, a style that became very popular. Depending on the peak of the roof, one could deter-

mine the social level of the family who lived underneath it. Limousin roofs have also been made into conical shapes topped by a ball or bird evocative of the Gallic rooster. Made with bumps or holes, these roof ornaments would whistle in the wind to frighten away evil spirits that might try to invade the house.

THE ENAMELS OF LIMOGES

Enamel appeared in the Limousin during the first half of the 13th century, thanks to the region's favorable soil conditions that provided an abundance of metals required for enamel-making. The region also boasts a long history of metal-working. Saint Eligius (588–660), the patron of goldsmiths, and a native of the region, established an atelier at the monastery of Solignac, just south of Limoges. But it was the nearby Grandmont Abbey, noted for its riches, that provided the patrons and religious connections that earned Limoges enamels worldwide attention.

During the 12th and 13th centuries, monks of the abbey initiated a campaign to decorate their sanctuary and house the abbey's relics using Limoges enamels. Word of the beauty of these enam-

els reached the English King Henry II, sovereign of the Limousin following his marriage in 1152 to Eleanor of Aquitaine. The couple became benefactors of the abbey and, through their connections and personal relations with England and the rest of Europe, helped to widen the market for Limoges enamels.

Enamels from Limoges decorated the churches and cathedrals of Western Europe and became so renowned they were given the Latin name, "Opus Lemovicense," or "Work made in Limoges." Objects of Limoges enamel were set on altars, taken on pilgrimages and carried by popes and bishops. The gold-and-enamel tomb of Saint Peter in Rome is made of Limoges enamel, as were altars in the cathedrals of Spain.

Known for its rich palette, dominated by lapis lazuli blue, set against gold and copper surfaces, Limoges enamelwork was well crafted, well made and relatively inexpensive. Limoges enamels also had secular uses, as candlesticks, water basins, boxes for valuables and tombs for the wealthy bourgeoisie. Enamels were widely used for coats of arms, traditionally made of decorated metal.

Having all but disappeared during the 14th century, Limoges enamel made a comeback during the Renaissance before fading into history once again. The Art Deco movement of the 1920s and '30s saw a renewed interest in Limoges enamels; today many collectors look for works of that era.

In 1966 the Limousin Union of Master Enamelmakers helped launch renewed interest in enamels, an effort that culminated in the first International Exposition of Enamel Art in 1971 in Limoges. The expo proved so successful that it was subsequently held in Canada, Japan and Germany.

Since the mid-1970s the number of traditional workshops has declined. Today about 40 independent enamel artists, aged 40 to 70, remain productive. The future relies on their ability to interest a new generation of artisans and on the creation of new enamel objects for modern use.

ANOTHER WORLD-FAMOUS EXPORT:
LIMOUSIN CATTLE

Aside from its excellent water supply and far-reaching green, rolling hills, the Limousin region has become known for its prize-winning cattle. Bred not for size but for economy, Limousin cattle are a hearty, medium-sized breed that are resistant to colder temperatures. Animal researchers describe them as being one of the most efficient beef breeds in the world today, due largely to the high survival rate of calves.

Limousin cattle are exported to nearly all beef-producing countries, including Canada, which began importing the breed in 1968. The popularity of Limousin cattle spread quickly and today it is the fastest growing purebred breed in Canada.

The Flavor of the Limousin

The Limousin region is best known for its simple peasant fare, from hearty meat dishes to fabulous desserts that have won the attention of gastronomes the world over.

Located in the Massif Central, the Limousin is known for cooking that reflects "the frugal habits of local countrywomen using up leftovers and baking them into delicious, substantial dishes," according to French regional cooking expert Jean Ferniot.

The undisputed star of the Limousin table is a dessert— *clafoutis* (sometimes spelled without the final *s*). This is a fruit tart frequently made with the region's magnificent cherries. Traditionally, the pits of the cherries are not removed, creating somewhat of a diner's dilemma. Some modern recipes for *clafoutis* advise the cook to pit the cherries before placing them in the tart, but most opt for tradition and simply advise the host to "warn your guests." The historian Charles Dugue provides instructions for coping with a mouthful of pits:

"To truly savor (the *clafoutis*) . . . one must have lived in the area for at least three generations in order to understand how to effortlessly assemble in the mouth the innumerable black cherries which constitute the foundation of this pastry. Much like the wave which rolls the pebbles on the beach of the Antarctic Sea, the tongue of the skillful eater of *clafoutis* rolls the pits against the rocky escarpments of the teeth, sucks them back against the cheeks, and divests them of their most delicious flesh."

Clafoutis

With or without pits, this is an easy dessert to prepare.

3 heaping tablespoons flour
2 eggs
salt
3¹/2 tablespoons sugar
I cup whole milk, at room temperature
3 tablespoons heavy cream
¹/2 teaspoon vanilla (optional)
I tablespoon butter
I¹/2 lb. sour cherries

Preheat oven to 325°

Mix together the flour, eggs, pinch of salt, and 3 tablespoons of the sugar in a medium-size bowl. Slowly add the milk, cream and vanilla (if using), stirring well.

Butter a 9" porcelain quiche dish or baking pan and heat in a warm oven, about 3 minutes.

Remove heated pan from oven, add cherries to create a bottom layer, and top with the custard mixture.

Bake for 45 minutes or until golden brown. Remove from oven and immediately sprinkle top with remaining sugar. Allow sugar to set. Serve while still warm.

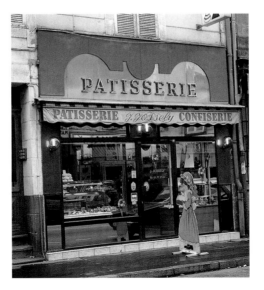

Porcelain tiles line the top of Les Halles (above left), the covered market of Limoges.

The superb cattle raised in the Limousin produce an undisputedly high quality beef. Limousin pork is also renowned; in fact, the fat of the pig, in addition to grains and chestnuts, is one of three basic elements of Limousin regional cooking.

If you spot an item on a menu listed as "*Carré de porc `a la limousine*," you can count on pork accompanied by red cabbage braised with chestnuts, another specialty of the region. Gastronome Waverly Root, however, claims that the "most famous single dish having its origin in the Limousin is *lièvre "à la royale*," or hare "fit for a king." This very old recipe was so popular in the 18th century that a specially-shaped earthenware dish was created for the sole purpose of cooking it.

Grains in the Limousin are commonly eaten as bread, buckwheat pancakes, and porridge prepared with flour and milk.

Chestnuts are considered such a treasure in these parts, the Regional Council has made its leaves part of its logo. Introduced by the Romans, chestnuts are traditionally eaten from October to March, sometimes as late as May. Locals blanch, grill or boil them. A simple but interesting soup featuring Limousin chestnuts is *Soupe aux marrons.*

Born of the Ancien Régime

The origins of the soup tureen are the same as the snuffbox; they are both French, born during the ancien régime. Like the snuffbox, the tureen became a fashionable collectible as the taste for French design, culture and art spread throughout Europe. But unlike the fans and wigs and ruffled shirts for men, the tureen was one fad that would survive well past the 18th century.

In those days, aristocratic and royal hosts were required to come up with extravagant tableware reflecting their good taste and financial success. The lavishly decorated tableware, combined with serving the meal *à la française,* when all courses were set upon the table at once in a sumptuous display, created a dramatic effect.

Like much of the richly, sometimes garishly decorated objects of the times, it was generally understood that the more exorbitant the display, the better.

There were soup tureens inspired by Roman antiquities and the highly romanticized bucolic scenes that were so popular during that time; there were also tureens in the shape of livestock and farm produce, swans, rabbits, a head of cabbage, a hen and chicks. Like other cherished pieces of formal dinnerware, tureens were made of porcelain, but also of faïence and earthenware.

Besides its decorative appeal, the tureen also served another social function. It ushered in the ritual of having soup as a first course, a tradition that would last to the end of the 19th century.

The Greeks and Romans were the first to fatten pigs, sows and geese so as to enlarge the livers of these animals. Once the liver was removed it would be soaked in milk and honey to further increase its size. The French first favored cock's or hen's liver and later developed a taste for fattened goose liver, known today as foie gras.

SUPERSTITION AND SPIRITUALITY
OF THE LIMOUSIN

Most residents of the Limousin region lead dual lives when it comes to their spirituality. While most are Christian, they can also be followers of the occult, preserving centuries' old rituals and superstitions.

CATHOLIC TRADITIONS: Since 1512, festivities in connection with a founding or venerated saint or the exposition of their relics have taken place every 7 years during the 50 days from Easter to Pentecost. Though the events are religious in nature, they do attract believers and nonbelievers alike. The elaborate public ritual includes the blessing of official festival flags, which are hoisted to bell towers and placed at the town's entrances, and a procession along the traditional, sacred route.

Water, which has been a symbolic part of Limoges village life for centuries, also plays a powerful role in local superstitions. Devoted to their saints, Limousin natives believe that certain fountains contain holy water that can provide cures and good luck. At Beaune Les Mines, near Limoges, hundreds of motorists and motorcyclists come to have their vehicles blessed on Saint Christopher's Day. Even military vehicles have been known to await the priests' blessings.

SORCERERS AND WITCHES: In addition to traditional Church doctrine, some in the Limousin also believe in the power of healers or sorcerers ("les sorciers") who are able to "lift" spells.

During the 16th century, the region seems to have witnessed its own version of the Salem Witch Hunt, in which several persons, including a priest called Aupetit, were accused of witchcraft. As recently as 1963, an alleged witch from Chateauponsac, known for starting tractors by using salt, was accused of creating havoc in a family. She was brought into court and the fiasco attracted the national media. Guilt or innocence, however, was never determined, as the trial eventually ended with the 70-year-old woman's death by natural causes.

SUPERNATURAL CREATURES: Limousin folklore also features a host of fantastic beings: A man who made a deal with the devil would be turned into a "loup-garou" (werewolf) and would run around the Limousin region at night, especially during the full moon, frightening and tormenting people and eating all the dogs in his path. The werewolf was compelled to include a tour of 9 churches, bell towers or communities. Exhausted by his nightly escapades, the *loup garou* sometimes liked to be carried by passersby and lick their faces to thank them. In exchange for all this havoc, the devil would grant the werewolf special privileges, such as creating a hailstorm or drying up cow's milk.

The devil, called "sifer" from "Lucifer," usually appeared as a big cat, dog, sheep or ram. Meeting him in one of these forms on a road was a bad omen.

The devil also had subordinates to help him in his evil-ways:

"*Les Danseurs de Nuit*" were young men or women who would innocently invite you to dance under the moonlight. They would then spit flames from their mouths, open the ground from under you and suck you into the earth.

"*Les Fées,*" or fairies, were other women who danced at night, all dressed in white. Seemingly innocent, they were known to tear off the limbs of children they caught.

"*Lutins*" were goblins no larger than a big cat and known to enter stables at night, braid all the hairs on the horses' manes, then make them run around outside all night long, making them too tired to work during the day. "*Lutins*" had a silver paw they would use to knock out the curious who came too close.

"*Fadettes*" were fairies with the torsos of women and goats' legs who lived in caves on the banks of the Vienne. They enjoyed scaring men, tormenting animals, turning milk sour, making hens unable to lay eggs and messing up the insides of homes.

"*Les Martes,*" brunette women with bare arms, breasts falling to their knees and thick hair to the ground, specialized in terrorizing farmers.

"*Les Vieilles*" (the old women) were

female demons who tormented people in their dreams. They could pass through keyholes and would smother dreamers to death by sleeping over them. Other *"vieilles"* would wait at the bottom of wells and under river beds and would drag in children who looked down into them.

"Les Revenants" and *"Les âmes en peine"* were ghosts and souls in pain who were trapped in purgatory and came back to earth to visit and haunt people.

"Les Laveuses de Nuit" or "night women washers" were the souls of women who had been condemned to clean laundry (which would never get clean and turn white) only at night by moonlight. They had been punished for bad acts committed during their lifetimes.

Legend has it that if headache sufferers were to soak their shirts in the waters of this stream and, after placing the shirts over their heads, were to hang their shirts over this cross, they would leave their headaches behind.

PART FOUR

The Return
of the Porcelain Box

The Birth of
a Box

The Return of the Porcelain Box

As in the 19th century, Americans continue to be the chief consumers of Limoges porcelain, except today the emphasis has shifted from tableware to boxes. One industry expert estimates that the U.S. market for boxes has expanded 500 percent in the past 5 years. Jean-Paul Marquet, the president and CEO of the 224-year-old Manufacture La Reine, offers another, although less impressive figure: he claims that the box-making business has more than doubled in the past 5 years. "The demand is so great, new companies have been popping up," Monsieur Marquet explains. To keep up, manufacturers are spending a lot of time and money on new designs. At La Reine, more than half of their production is devoted to new designs. The goal: to please the growing numbers of collectors who continually seek new pieces.

Fortunately, snuff has gone the way of the powdered

wig, but these tiny porcelain containers have lived on in styles no self-respecting 18th-century fop could have imagined, encompassing an amazing array of designs. From time to time a box will still be enlisted to hold a treasured object— one California man presented his loved one with an engagement ring inside—but more often today's boxes are admired for their beauty alone.

Collecting contemporary Limoges porcelain boxes is a relatively recent phenomenon, though one that is rapidly growing. Up until the mid-1960s, such high-quality hand-painted collectibles were virtually nonexistent. At that time, only a handful were to be found in Limoges, but only in traditional shapes—round, square and rectangular. Among the first importers who brought Limoges porcelain boxes to the United States were Charles Martine Inc. (Chamart) and Rochard.

Some believe the red roof tiles of Limoges, which are still made today,

earned the city its nickname "La Ville Rouge."

A New Collectible

During the mid-1970s, Richard Sonking, the president of Rochard, an importer of Limoges porcelain based in New York, discovered a new collection of boxes at a workshop owned by Robert Piotet. Monsieur Piotet had encountered the 18th-century snuffboxes in museum collections and, inspired by their charm, began creating a line of about 12 relatively large (about 3- to 4-inch) animal boxes, including pheasants, ducks, horses and pigs. Mr. Sonking was immediately intrigued.

"There was something so special about them," Mr. Sonking recalls. "I was drawn to their detail, to the characteristics of the animal shapes, and the high level of workmanship."

Up until that time, Rochard, which Mr. Sonking had founded in 1972 with his father, Herbert, and brother-in-law, Roger Fargeon, had been importing traditional dinnerware service as well as giftware, bath accessories, perfume trays and hand-painted faïence cookware. Taking on these miniature boxes was not without risk—after all, these boxes really had no modern use other than as decoration—but they were nevertheless captivating and unique.

"I was intrigued by the size of the boxes and by the porcelain itself—its glossy and smooth contours," he explains. "When you add the delicate hand-painting and the element of the hinging, I knew this was a wonderful item. Just opening the box and hearing it close with a little click was so magical."

Mr. Sonking was sure that if he had been smitten, others would be too. "These boxes were so different from anything I had seen, I thought others would think so too."

Fortunately, Mr. Sonking's instincts were right. As a result, Rochard was one of the first companies to introduce hand-painted Limoges boxes to the United States. Dorothy Adams was among the early enthusiasts who helped create a demand for Limoges boxes.

Rochard's First Collection.

"They were immediately appealing to me because I could see they would attract people with so many different lifestyles," says Dorothy Adams, who, when president of Gump's By Mail, featured boxes in their catalogues between 1987–96. "If you collect dogs you could choose a dog. If you go to the movies you can buy a bag of popcorn in porcelain or if you love the ballet there are ballet slippers. There's literally something for everyone."

THE FIRST FULL COLLECTION

Shortly afterward, in the mid-1970s, Rochard began working with a small studio headed by Liliane Fouquet, who had started creating small animals (one and a half to two inches long), unusual forms such as pears and apples and traditional geometric shapes. Fouquet, too, had been inspired by the 18th-century *tabatières* she had seen in museums and wanted to recreate their charm. They became the nucleus of Rochard's collection of Limoges boxes.

John Curran, vice-president of merchandising and special publications at the Metropolitan Museum of Art in New York, first encountered Limoges boxes while at the Kenton Collection, which became the Horchow Collection, a mail-order gift catalogue.

"They were charming and very good mail-order products," he explains. "There was a history to them and they are often commemorative. They were also very appealing to women, who make up the majority of the gift market."

Gradually, what began as a small grouping of boxes grew steadily as they became more popular. By the mid-1980s, the demand for boxes increased dramatically, spurring a number of innovative styles and concepts.

As more and more collectors began to discover the joys of accumulating these miniatures, competition among producers grew. New factories sprang up, fueling the creative end of the business even further. "At that point we had to decide which factories would give us the quality we wanted and work only with them," says Mr. Sonking.

Rochard's First Collection.

Professional designers create preliminary sketches, such as these by Julia Grant,
as the first step in the creation of a box.

INNOVATIVE DESIGN—FROM THE START

As often happens in art, the idea for a box can come from unexpected places—an image glimpsed in a photograph, a museum or a secondhand shop.

Many of the first contemporary boxes were inspired by the *tabatières* of the 18th- century. Reproductions continue to be pop-ular today. Mr. Curran introduced Limoges boxes a year after he joined the Metropolitan Museum in 1992. In 1997 their mail-order catalogue featured 6 such boxes; its main museum shop, from 25–30; and satellite shops, from 10–12. Some of them are 18th- and 19th-century reproductions; the rest are inspired by objects in the museum's Costume Institute. "They run the

Where Boxes are Made

There are three types of operations, with some variations, involved in the making of a Limoges porcelain box.

Studios: Usually a family business, studios generally consist of two or three people who work out of a small workshop or home office. Typically, such studios decorate porcelain whiteware, or blanks, purchased from factories, which is why the same shape may be seen with different decorations. Sometimes the skills of additional decorators, also home-based, are employed before the box is sent off to be hinged and mounted.

Ateliers: Employing anywhere from 5 to 20 workers, ateliers not only decorate but frequently hinge the boxes as well. Sometimes they employ full-time model makers who produce whiteware and who sometimes work with an independent sculptor.

Factories: Since the early days of the Haviland company, factories conduct every aspect of box-making, from mold-making to decoration and hinging. Factories employ anywhere from 40–200 workers and also sell whiteware to ateliers and studios for decoration.

gamut—from the more refined little box with pretty flowers to a little box in the shape of a mouse," he explains.

Sometimes designers use antique boxes as starting points, but after modifications the result may be something totally different. Others are more skilled at conceiving boxes that are completely new, taking their cues from everyday life. These innovators have produced ingenious forms that are both novel and new. And not all of these ideas come from professional designers.

Mr. Sonking, for example, conceived of the idea for several boxes. After once seeing a brilliant red chili pepper while flipping through the pages of a magazine, he thought it would make a great box. It did. Today the chili peppers, one in green and

another in yellow, have become tremendously popular because they are realistic and whimsical. Another idea for a box came after Mr. Sonking spotted a wonderfully shaped silver hippopotamus on a visit to the Hermitage in St. Petersburg.

Professional designers are also employed to create new boxes and Rochard works with several of them both here and abroad. The factories themselves also conceive of ideas for new boxes.

"The factories are a wonderful source of creativity," says Mr. Sonking. "The competitiveness of the business has created the need and opportunity for factories to be creative. We are constantly collaborating to introduce new styles and designs."

Since Rochard works with a number of factories or workshops, each with its own specialty, Rochard determines which would be best to create a desired effect. Sometimes the skills of numerous design studios are employed. These relation-

ships give Rochard a great deal of creative flexibility that results in an extremely diverse assortment. "If we worked with only one factory in Limoges our collection today wouldn't be as comprehensive as it is," Mr. Sonking adds.

"What distinguishes Rochard from other companies is that they've been in the forefront of product development," adds Ms. Adams, who continues to promote Rochard boxes in the Charles Keath mail-order catalogue of gift, home and fashion items, where she is senior vice president of marketing and merchandising. "Rochard has a good working relationship with the factories so you get the best quality and what's brand new."

This relationship, which allows creativity to flow—creates a good situation for everyone involved. Mr. Sonking explains: "It's good for the artist and it's good for the collector because he or she truly gets a miniature work of art."

Black-bottom pigs, so common to the Limousin region,
provided the inspiration for these boxes.

The Birth of a Box

The making of a porcelain box continues to be a manual process that has remained unchanged for more than 100 years. Only the techniques of firing have been updated. The electricity and gas now used to fire the kilns have eliminated the need for *flotteurs de bois, hommes du four, engazetiers* and *enfourneurs. Moulins à pâte* are now called *fabricants de pâte,* where the porcelain paste is produced. There are few *useurs de grains,* but their skills continue to be called upon whenever a defect has to be smoothed out by hand. After firing, molds are still manually carved, the porcelain is still hand-poured and each piece of bisque is filed and polished by hand. The long tradition of hand-painting continues, but only the designation of the artists has changed, from *artistes en porcelaine* to *deco-*

Porcelain paste arrives at factories in the form of large pallets.

rateurs en porcelaine. Moufles continue to be used to set the paints and mounting is still done by hand.

"No machines are used at all," Mr. Sonking explains. That's why Rochard boxes are as precious as they are, but more importantly, it's why they look the way they do. No two pieces will ever be identical. And that's great news for collectors. They will always have an original.

"In a world where everything is made very quickly and time is measured in nanoseconds and how many pieces can be done in an hour, most companies are figuring out how they can reduce labor costs," explains Mr. Sonking. "It's refreshing to come across an exquisite objet d'art which is done entirely by hand. A machine can't replace what the hand can paint. Everything about the process—from the original sketch to the fitting of the hinge—is entirely handmade."

And labor intensive it is. One industry expert estimates that about 30 steps are necessary—and as many as 12 people—to craft a product that can fit into the palm of one's hand. At the Manufacture La Reine in Limoges, 4 people are involved in working on the "blank"; 2 on decor; 3 to 4 on hinging; 1 on quality control and 1 for packaging.

The creation of a box is indeed a labor of love, but the painstaking work is a labor nonetheless. To understand just how intensive it is, let us take a look at the process involved in making a Limoges porcelain box.

The first step in the porcelain process is developing pastes or powders. Depending on the type of product to be created and how it will be shaped, either one or the other is selected. In keeping with the mystery and competitive nature that has surrounded the

Here the paste is shaped into logs
to be made into saucers.

making of porcelain since its early days, each manufacturer has its own secret recipe and is quite tight-lipped about revealing it. No matter what proportions they may use, manufacturers use the following basic ingredients:

• Kaolin adds whiteness and pliancy. Highly resistant to heat, kaolin does not melt and gives the object its shape.

• Quartz gives porcelain its translucent quality.

• Petunse, a type of feldspar, is the melting element necessary to help fuse the ingredients into a glass-like end product.

Once the paste or powder is made, porcelain is variably shaped, depending on the type of object to be created.

Calibration is a process reserved for circular-shaped pieces such as plates and round platters. The outside of the calibrated object is made on a plaster mold that creates its interior shape. Melting is a process used for complicated pieces, such as coffee-pots, soup bowls and hollow containers such as boxes. Isostatic pressing is a technique recently adopted to create flat pieces and is being used more and more frequently to make more complicated forms. Used as a replacement for the calibration process, it involves using dried granules that are subjected to equal amounts of pressure in all directions. Once the shapes are created by any of these methods, firing and decorating follow.

Surface modifications can entail carving, perforating and embossing or applying a relief design, which is usually molded separately and attached to the porcelain. A method of embossing called "slip" involves the application of water and clay to the item with a brush.

Painting begins with the application of a colored glaze, such as the well-known Chinese celadon, or underglaze, designs painted on a piece before it is glazed. The most widely used underglaze is a deep cobalt blue found on many objects made in China and Europe. Paints applied over the glaze are commonly called enamels; made from metallic oxides of iron, copper and magnesium, these paints require a second firing to become permanent.

Creating a porcelain box requires more artistry than a simple piece of tableware. Boxes are more sculptural, their shapes more variable in design from year to year, and require more custom painting, in miniature, no less. Moreover, boxes have additional details—a hinge and a latch—that have to be precisely designed and mounted. From conception to finished product, the following describes the making of a Limoges porcelain box:

Creation

Start with a photograph or a drawing, as Jean-Pierre Bonnet is doing. Here he sculpts the plaster shape. From the plaster shape the sample mold is made again in plaster.

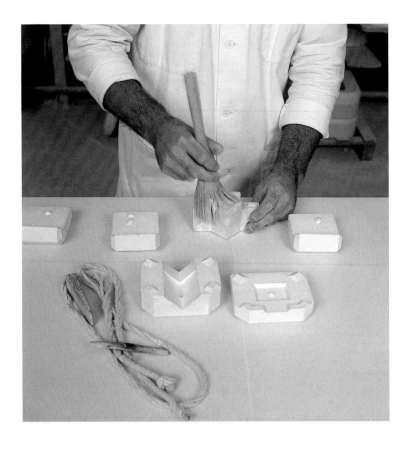

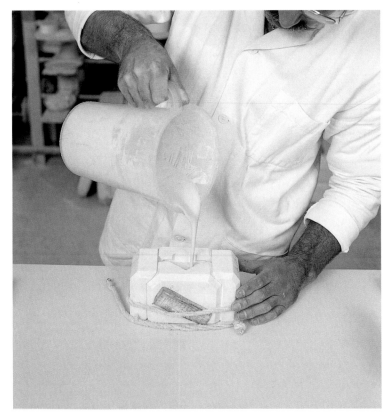

From the sample mold, David Gavinet makes the matrix with a harder plaster. In the photo above, he greases the mold, prior to pouring the plaster. At bottom right, he unmolds the matrix.

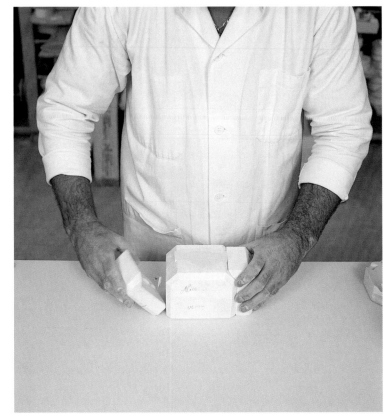

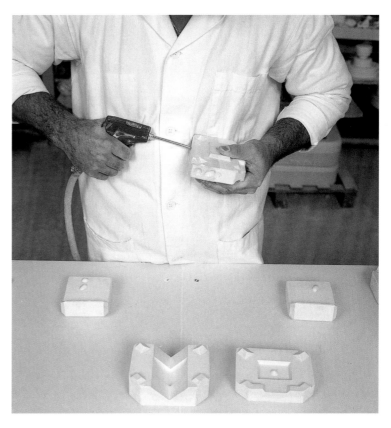

Then, from the matrix, a casting mold
is made in plaster. This final mold is carefully engineered to be
more durable (above). The more intricate the box,
the more parts to the mold (left).

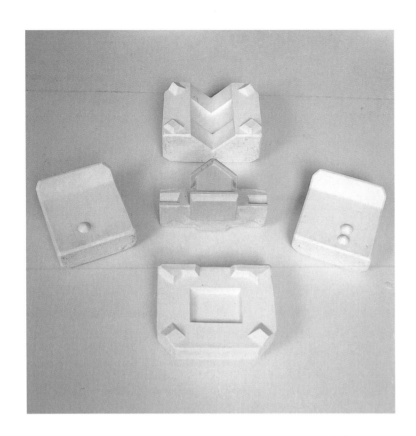

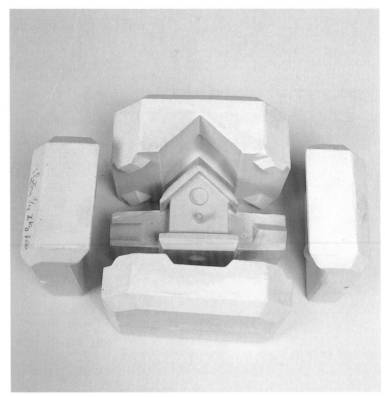

The casting mold is unveiled.

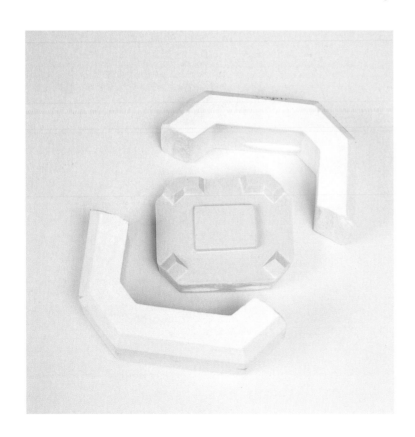

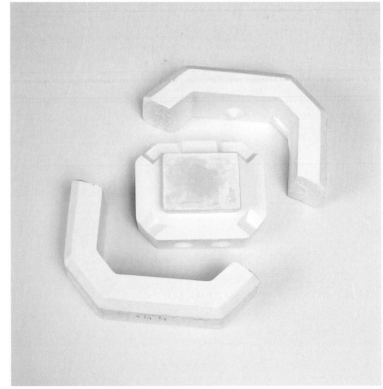

Manufacturing the Blank

Alain Desmoulin feeds a paste pallet into the vat where it will liquify before being poured into the molds.

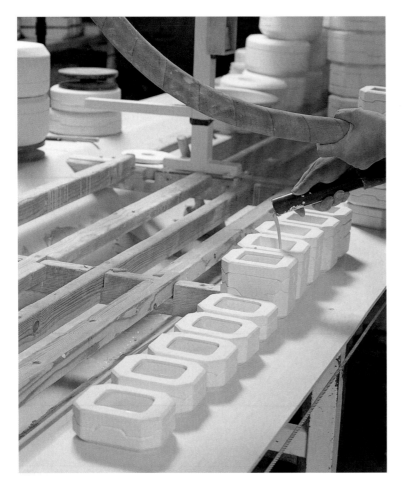

Liquid porcelain paste, or "barbotine," is poured

into the molds by Nicole Peyronnet.

Here she unmolds the pieces.

The pieces are set aside to dry for a minimum of 24 hours.

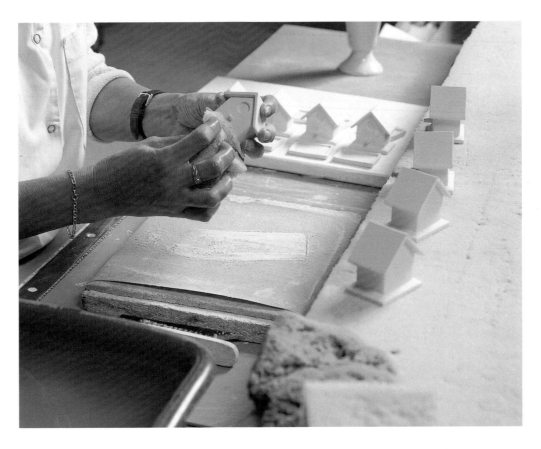

Jeanine Chaussadas removes excess clay with a sponge and knife.

Firing at 980° C (1796° F).

Before the piece is glazed it needs to be cleaned and stamped "Limoges."

Glazing (dipping in a glazing liquid). Glazing is often still done by hand, a process
that can be beautifully executed. Some glazers, such as Lucette Pironaud, can cover the entire object
with one dramatic wave of the hand.
Next, the excess glaze is removed from the edges and the feet of the box
before being fired again at 1400° C (2552° F).

Decoration

After firing, the pieces are carefully sorted before being painted. Muriel Mazeau applies
the colors with a brush. Gold details are applied with great delicacy and the tiniest of brushes. Typically, porcelain must be
fired after each color application, as shown here, at petit feu ("low fire"—a lower temperature) to set the colors.

Mounting and Hinging

A custom process, mounting begins as a
long piece of metal is shaped to fit each box, as Jacques
Pougeaud illustrates. Because each box is unique, each piece of
metal must be individually shaped directly onto the box.

The hinge is soaked in an acid solution
to give it an antiqued effect. (This step is omitted if a brilliant
shine is desired.) Artisans must keep track of mountings to make
sure each is returned to its proper box.

The hinge is glued around the edges of the box
and the hinge and clasp are adjusted
to make for a perfect fit.

FROM THE ARTIST'S HAND TO YOU: A BOX IS PAINTED BY A MASTER

Painters require 3 years' training before they can set brush to porcelain. The minimum required to become a master is 10 years.

Jean-Luc Soulat is a master painter with his own workshop who shares with us here the process of turning a white porcelain box into a miniature work of art. This footed, shaped box, in the "Basket of Cherries" design, is part of Rochard's limited-edition Studio Collection.

Once a motif is designed, I apply the pattern to the lid and to the bottom of the box. This is an ancient way of creating a motif: you reproduce the drawing on tracing paper which, after having been placed upside down on a thick cloth, is then daintily perforated all along the lines of the motif. The tool I use for perforating is a *piquoire*, a thin wooden instrument with a sewing needle at one end.

After this long and delicate process, I can see that the tracing paper or *poncif* has created some pinholes. Each of those small craters will allow the passage of a powdered coloring that will come to reproduce in *pointillisme* the motif to be traced.

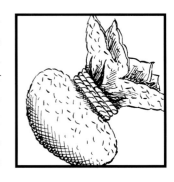

I rub a piece of charcoal on the surface of sandpaper to create the powdered coloring. A cotton ball, called *poncette*,

wrapped in velvet proves to be the ideal tool to apply the charcoal powder. Any excess of the black powder can simply be blown away with a puff of breath. What is left will be a discreet guide for the creation of the motif's lines. The char-

coal marks of the pattern will vanish in the oven during the first firing session.

Once the pattern is made, I will be able to use it another 50 to 80 times; after that another one will have to be made.

STEP ONE: LINE DRAWING, SIGNATURE AND MARKING

The thin, powdered black paint is diluted with water. Confectioners' sugar must be added to create an adhesive that will make it stick to the porcelain. This mixture favors the use of a *plume éffilée* (sharp-pointed pen), which will allow me to achieve fine and precise lines.

It is important to take any oil off the porcelain before applying the pattern, or else the pleasure of tracing the drawing turns into a trying effort. The paint will not take on the slippery material that is porcelain.

It is at this same stage that the two pieces of the box are numbered and that the stamp as well as the origin are written underneath.

Thus made, this first essential step will be fixed by firing.

Placed into the oven at night, the porcelain boxes decorated with their drawings will be subjected for three hours to increasing temperatures until the necessary 800° C (1472° F) mark is reached. They will then be slowly cooled down until morning to approximately 15° C (59° F) and be taken out of the kiln.

STEP TWO: APPLYING THE FIRST COLOR

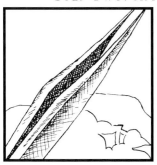

The entire motif: cherries, basket and insects, as well as the raised relief of the box's feet, are covered with a special varnish that transforms itself while drying into a compact layer that can be taken off with *pince fine* (thin tweezers). This varnish serves to protect the details on the motif and the feet. At this point, I can apply the yellow paint on the background without danger of coloring the motif. This yellow paint, like the others that will be used, is prepared on a glass or porcelain plaque with the help of a spatula that is called a *couteau à palette* (see page 170). Turpentine and oily turpentine (turpentine made thicker by evaporation) constitute the two dilution elements of the powdered paints for porcelain.

I select a square brush made of *petit gris* (squirrel hair) to put tint on the porcelain. The brush is flat, half-size, approximately 1 centimeter wide and square at the end (see page 171). The next step is to paint the color yellow as evenly as possible, then to immediately

and softly dab the paint with a small fine-grained sponge to distribute it evenly. I use the *pince fine* again to help remove the protective film that constitutes the special varnish.

After a drying period of a couple of hours either out of the oven or even more rapidly if left inside, the first tints can be put on this rustic motif. For the basket, I apply a brownish-red color in one thin layer. The cherries are done in purple-pink, purple-ruby and dark purple. These last three tints owe their luminosity to the addition of gold to the color mixtures.

I color the leaves in "prairie green." Other tints such as "buttercup yellow," "Parma violet," "chestnut brown," "iron red" and

"Pompadour pink" will be used to color the butterflies and insects that are attracted by the sweetness of the fruits overflowing from the small basket.

The brushes I have chosen for this first step of coloring the motif are round in shape, a little full and not too thin. They are called *grain de blé* (wheat grain) brushes. Thinner brushes will be used to paint the cherries and insects. A thicker brush will yield better results for the basket.

Once this work is done, the pieces are put in the kiln for a firing at 770° C (1428° F). It is not until early the next morning that we will be able to judge the result of this creation. At that point more work will be required.

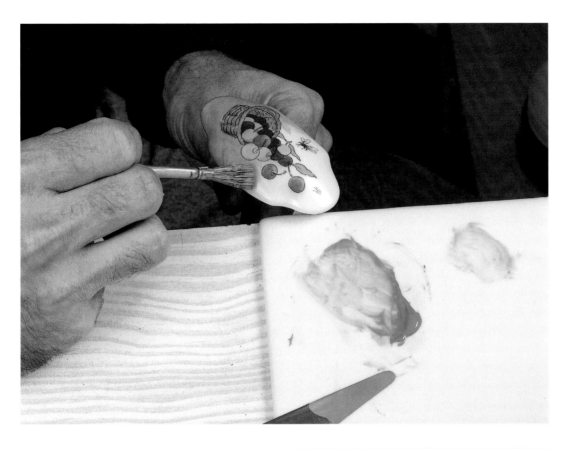

STEP THREE:
ADDING GRAY TO THE
COLORED BACKGROUND

Once again I must cover the motif, the insects and the feet of the box with the special varnish. The *gris fleur* ("flower gray") powdered paint must be diluted with more oily turpentine to get a pretty shade of gray on the yellow background. I use a square brush in *petit gris* to put the tint on, and the desired effect is obtained by using the small fine-grained sponge.

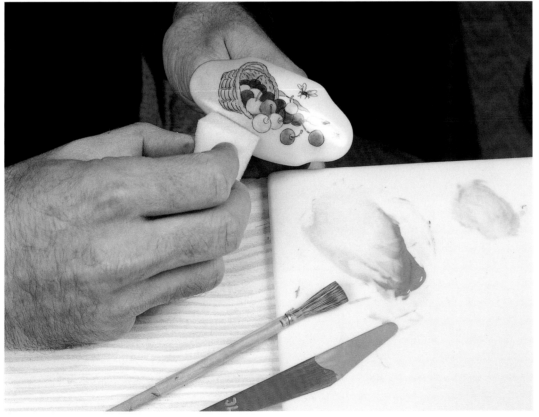

STEP FOUR:
SECOND STEP OF ADDING
COLORS TO THE MOTIF
AND MATTE GOLD
ON THE FEET

When the *gris fleur* ("flower gray") is perfectly dry, a second color coating must be put on the whole of the motif. The same tints as the ones for the sketch will be used. This time it is essential to intensify the tones, especially in the shadows. For the basket I must underline well each part of the weave. The cherries are more delicate to handle; their tints must be painted in a well-controlled circular movement. It is the sense of contrast on each cherry that will give the whole picture a vivid, raised-relief effect.

Sometimes I find it necessary to hold my breath to get the exact paint stroke. The mind must no longer wander and a high degree of concentration is required. Creating the crispness of the swollen fruits is a rewarding part of the effort, equal to the pleasure of creating the cherries with the strokes of the paintbrush.

The tool I'm using here is a *pinceau à décor* (a decorating brush), round, half-size, with a short point. The brush is also made from *petit gris*, and, like others made from sable and skunk hair,

all come from actual furs whose costs fluctuate with the rhythms of the stock market.

The feet in raised relief at the bottom of the box have to be painted in gold. This step also requires a *pinceau à décor* but this one will be a little more fleshy, allowing me to use more paint. The gold is called "matte gold at 30%," a semi-oily liquid, dark brown in color, and 30 percent pure gold. This brown color must be applied together with the colors outlining the raised relief feet of the box. It must cover well the parts which need to be painted gold.

Firing at 700° C (1292° F) sets the paints and brings out the gold of a work that already starts to take on a very beautiful aspect.

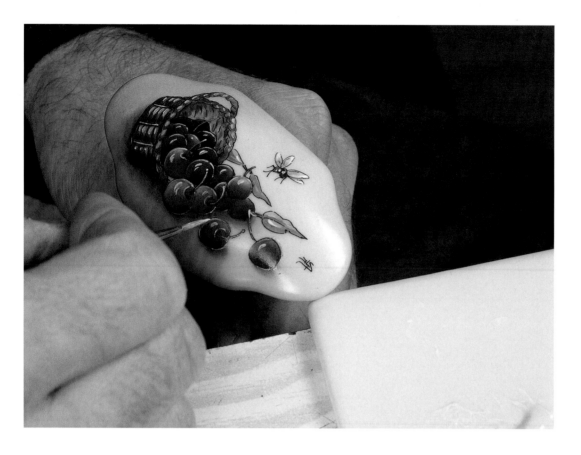

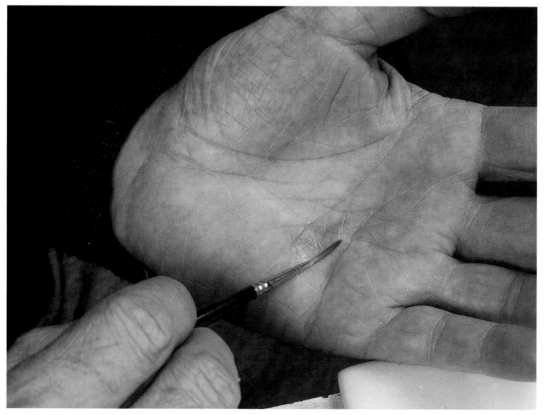

STEP FIVE: THIRD STEP IN COLORING MOTIF AND 'REPIQUE' OF LINES ON GOLD FEET

Sometimes, in the morning, I happen to pick up boxes that are still too hot. It is because I am impatient to continue working on them, to get them to the final stage, a stage that I wish to be both poetic and realistic. Patience is a virtue! In any case, hot porcelain dries up paint before I have obtained the desired effect from the paintbrush.

We are now at a stage of the work where it is difficult to find terms corresponding to the precise gestures. One must use one's feeling to bring out the richness of the tints. It is not yet the final stage but an additional step where each detail outlined will enhance the contrasts of the entire piece. One must be careful not to make the color too thick, which would darken the motif and could provoke *l'écaillage* (scaling or chipping) of the paint, which has already been fired three times.

It is time to strengthen the shadows on the ground to highlight the basket and cherries. The floating effect on a background of uniformed tint will disappear and the motif will come more to life.

The gold on the raised relief of the feet has taken on a beautiful color during the firing session. Its surface is matte. On this base I trace with a *pinceau à repique* the mounting of the 3 cherries and the 4 veined leaves that make up each foot. This *pinceau à repique* is thin, long and fragile with a brush made from *petit gris*.

The chestnut-brown powdered paint is diluted to be made a little oily. It is highly recommended that the paint be prepared in advance; the day before is ideal. This waiting period will give it certain qualities that will give the brush a dense and neat line without any unsteadiness when making a fast movement.

A medium firing temperature of 750° C (1382° F) will combine all the differently created tint layers with this last very delicate one.

STEP SIX: ADDING THE FINISHING TOUCHES IN WHITE AND BROWN 'APPLATS' (SHADES) ON THE GOLD OF THE FEET

The work is now at its most advanced stage. Even though the entire body of the work has an agreeable look, I want everything to be perfect. I want to add details to the lighting effect of this spring motif.

I therefore choose a sable hair *pinceau de finition* (finishing brush), half long and fine, with a well-formed tip. It will be used to put

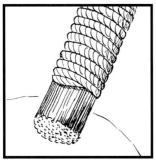

on the white finishing paint in thin layers with some highlights. This powder is also to be diluted with turpentine, to which some oily turpentine must be added.

The required precision goes hand in hand with the slowness of the gesture that a sufficiently thick layer of paint demands. I add a fine brown shadow to the cherries and golden leaves of the four feet. Since the motif inside the box is a reflection of the design on the lid, it also must be given its finishing tints.

The entire work will undergo a final firing at 740° C (1364° F).

The boxes finally come out of the oven, never to return there again. At the last stage of this labor of love, one must not forget to make the matte gold of the feet shine. In effect, during its first firing, the gold became a fine matte layer that masked its shine. It is now useful to eliminate this veneer, to give the 24-carat gold its most beautiful aspect. One must use a circular motion to brush the surface of the gold matte using a *gratte bosse*, a cylinder of strongly fastened, fine fiberglass. The hinge can now be put on this finished piece of work.

Created with studied elegance and passion, my works leave the artist's studio of Lemovice, like many silent yet expressive messages, toward unknown eyes and hands that my creations dream of seducing.

PART FIVE

A Style
for Every Taste

Today Rochard carries over 1,000 styles of Limoges porcelain boxes. Each year, between 200 to 300 new boxes make their debut at the spring and fall trade shows in New York. Of Rochard's complete line of boxes, 98 percent are entirely hand-painted.

The following is a chronological overview of some of the categories introduced by Rochard—including the innovations that have made them famous.

Mennecy (1748–1806) walnut box.

ANIMALS

Inspired by 18th-century French tabatières found in the museums of Europe, these were the first boxes introduced by Rochard in the mid-1970s. The first, including a pheasant, lovebirds and a frog, were a larger size, three to three and a half inches long.

Next came smaller pieces, one- to two- inches long, in the shapes of a rooster, duck and lovebirds. Today, animals as a category have grown to include well over 100 styles. Boxes range from the serious, realistically detailed endangered animal series to a whimsical collection featuring a pig in a bathtub and bears on a seesaw. For cat and dog lovers, there are many breeds and varieties. The pug, the favored pet of the ancien régime, can be found on boxes based on 18th-century originals.

TRADITIONAL

*R*ochard's first complete box collection in the mid-1970s contained
a number of traditional geometric shapes, as well as the heart, treasure chest and
hat-pin box. These timeless styles have always been a part of the Rochard line,
even though their decoration and inspiration have changed over the years.

WHIMSICAL

During the late 1970s, Rochard was the first to introduce the idea of finding surprises inside boxes. Thimbles were the first surprises, found first within an upright egg. The next were more luxurious: a perfume bottle inside an egg, followed by a tiny chest that opened to reveal two perfume bottles with faux pearls on top. Variations on the theme included an egg and a heart, both containing a single perfume bottle topped with a faux pearl.

Spurred by new possibilities, Rochard quickly introduced several new novelty boxes of their own design. An antique glove box opened to reveal antique gloves; a hatbox contained a tiny porcelain hat; and a tiny watercolor paint box held a brush inside and was decorated with colored brush marks on the box.

More recent additions to this category are every bit as engaging, with each demanding a closer look. A box in the shape of an antique picnic basket contains two plates and two forks and knives. A metal chain holds the "basket" open. The French egg carton, one of the most intriguing of these boxes, opens up to reveal six miniature porcelain eggs, one of which is removable for inspection. Another fun box is the wooden champagne crate with a mini-replica of this famous French beverage inside.

FRUITS AND VEGETABLES

*T*he watermelon was the first in this category (1983), followed by the half-orange,
half-pear and half-apple, designed to reveal the seeds of each fruit in realistic detail; these were
introduced in the mid-1980s. A small carrot box, which opened up to reveal
a brown bunny, also made its debut.

BABY

*T*his is a large and popular category for Rochard, representing between 50 and 75 boxes to celebrate the birth of a child. Baby-inspired boxes made their debut in the mid-1980s. Styles range from a simple round box with a pink or blue decal to an elaborate crib, complete with metal mobile.

"We try to get collectors at an early age," Mr. Sonking jokes, but there's actually some truth to his statement. Some young collectors have started out with a first birthday box.

MUSICAL

This antique drum, circa 1765—1770, was the inspiration for the
Rochard design pictured on page 70.

*I*n 1990 a violin mounted on an oval shape
made its debut, followed by a mandolin and a piano.
More intricate porcelain instruments soon took
shape—the harp, French horn, mandolin and
free-standing violin—with as much realistic detail
and fine craftsmanship as their music-making
counterparts. More recent boxes feature instruments and their cases, including the violin, guitar
and saxophone. For rock-and-rollers, an electric
guitar is available.

SPORTS

*G*olf, tennis, fishing and horse-manship have been the most popular subjects for Rochard's sports-inspired boxes. Over the years there have been numerous golf bags, as well as golf balls, a tennis racquet, fishing creel, a boat with a casting fisherman, jockey cap, horse boxes, a horse jumping over a steeple and equestrian scenes. In addition to depicting the more genteel pastimes, such as billiards, Rochard has also turned current sports trends into design; its new "snow-boarding" box is a good example.

FLOWERS

In 1991, Rochard began a series of opened flowers, featuring petunias, pansies and poppies. Whole flowers, which were split in the middle and hinged, followed, along with nosegay flowers in flower pots and flower carts.

FOODS

*T*his category satisfies the food lover in all of us. Hamburgers, popcorn and a box of peanuts represent the all-American favorites, while foods with an international flavor include wheels of Brie or Camembert, a croissant, a bagette, foie gras and caviar.

A nostalgia for the past can be found in an old-fashioned bag of coffee beans, milk bottles, jams and canning jars of olives and cherries so detailed that a painted rubber ring can be seen between the jar and lid.

THE LIMITED EDITION STUDIO COLLECTION

*I*ntroduced in 1994, this special collection represents a quality of workmanship above and beyond Rochard's already high standards of painting and design. Using fine brush strokes and unusual painterly techniques, which can make the berries on a Christmas box appear three-dimensional, these boxes feature more colors, 15 to 20 rather than the usual 6 to 12, and liberal use of gold (24 carat), which has to be painted separately and fired separately.

Such painstaking details demand more time, are produced on a smaller scale and, as a result, cost a bit more. "We try to educate our customers as to why these are different," Mr. Sonking explains. "It's been quite successful for those collectors who can afford and want the best quality painting," adds Mr. Sonking. The "R.S. Collection" comes specially packaged in an elaborate hinged gift box and features an elegant scroll detailing the special workmanship involved.

Qu'est-ce que cela veut dire?
Making Sense of the Markings

Ninety-eight percent of Rochard boxes are hand-painted but others use a combination of decals and painting. To determine which is which, check the hand-painted inscriptions (usually underneath the box or under a lid) that are also indicators of quality and cost. Appropriately, the more handwork involved in making a box, the more expensive it will be.

In terms of markings by an individual factory or studio, there are inconsistencies because each studio has its own individual logo and not all of them regularly imprint it on boxes.

Here is a guide to the most common markings that describe the decorative process:

PEINT MAIN: *Hand-painted.* That means *all* of the painting on the box was done by hand.

REHAUSSÉ: *Enhanced by hand.* The box was probably decorated with decals that have been highlighted by hand-painting, adding dimension or relief.

DÉCORÉ MAIN: *Decorated by hand.* Usually found on a box that has been decorated solely with decals—by hand.

As a true limited edition, the RS Collection features 2 to 3 new designs every season (50 to 250 pieces of each), which are then discontinued. To date, 16 designs have been introduced, half of which have completely sold out.

What also distinguishes the RS Collection from other Rochard boxes is its emphasis on painting rather than form. Most of the shapes are classic, but every now and then an unusual form will come along—the most recent being an Empire sofa.

EXCLUSIVES

*R*ochard is often commissioned to create exclusive pieces for major retailers, specialty stores and corporations. Though some are not available to the public (since they are given as corporate gifts), they are nevertheless as captivating as the rest of the Rochard collection. The following is a sampling of some of these exclusive boxes:

Neiman Marcus: An ornately decorated egg featuring a floating butterfly inside, and a shopping bag and hatbox, decorated with the "NM" logo. In celebration of Stanley Marcus's book, *Minding the Store,* a miniature replica was made into a box.

Gump's: The powerful Asian influence in the City-by-the-Bay has inspired most of the boxes for this specialty store: a Chinese Fu dog, a symbol of good luck; a Buddha on a gold base; a replica of the emperor's palace; a pagoda; and a bowl of rice with chopsticks. One of the most recent boxes for Gump's makes for a tasteful souvenir: a replica of the Golden Gate Bridge.

Henri Bendel: A shopping bag in the brown-and-white stripe that is this New York boutique's trademark.

Nordstrom: Two boxes with the Nordstrom logos, each containing delightful surprises: porcelain truffles, one of which is removable, and a shoe box with a pair of removable black pumps.

Saks Fifth Avenue: a white-and-black shopping bag with the grand old store's logo.

What to Look for in a Box

Since the introduction of Limoges porcelain boxes to the U.S. in the mid-1970s, there have been scores of companies that have sprung up, hoping to profit from this extremely lucrative and competitive market. All boxes, however, are not created equal. With these helpful tips, provided by Richard Sonking of Rochard, and a discerning eye, one should be able to distinguish between a fine hand-painted piece and low-quality imitations.

COLOR: How many colors are being used? (Usually, the more colors applied, the more expensive the piece.) And do they complement the piece or detract from it?

DESIGN: Is the design carefully thought out? Does the design match the shape? Is the shape too small for the object—or too large? If companies scrimp on design, they are probably scrimping on other aspects of the process as well.

GILDING: If there is gold, is it brilliant or matte? Real gold (24- carat, the highest concentration of gold, is traditionally used) has a unique luster. Does the gilding work in harmony with the design or is it applied excessively to create a garish effect? (Gold adds to the price and quality because it requires an additional firing and because it has to be polished to achieve that shine.)

SHAPE: In a figure, for example, what does the face look like—is it well done? Can you see an eyelid or eyebrow, or is there merely a dot to represent an eye? Look for details in all of the shapes that signify that the creator has taken pains to impart realistic qualities that reflect a superior level of workmanship.

HINGE AND LATCH: There are about four or five degrees of quality. "We use the best," Mr. Sonking explains. (Almost all of Rochard's hinges and latches are of brass, which are either soaked in an acid wash to create an antique effect or polished to a brilliant shine. A few are gold plated.) Make sure the box opens and closes evenly and that the hinges and latches relate to the overall design. A golf-club box, for example, is appropriately decorated with a golf ball latch. That shows you that the designers have taken the time to think through important details—an indicator of quality.

• DETAIL: Mr. Sonking advises that the best boxes must meet the test of "the human eye." The closer you get to it, the better it should look.

• PAINTERLY TECHNIQUE: "In the final analysis the quality of the box is determined by the quality of the painting," Mr. Sonking explains. At most Limoges factories, painters don't set brush to box until garnering at least three years' experience. Pieces that are entirely hand-painted are the easiest to determine because they are painted over the glaze, have a texture when touched, and tiny brush strokes and irregularities that can be seen when examined closely. (See page 214 to understand the markings that identify the types of decoration used.)

PART SIX

The
Passion to
Collect

The excitement of discovering some new and fascinating detail with every glance, the desire to collect, display and continually marvel at the miniature beauty and excellence in craftsmanship describe the passionate collector of today's Limoges porcelain boxes. And there are growing numbers of enthusiasts all over the world who are filling shelves and display cabinets with these tiny collectibles. Among the luminaries who are known to have a passion for collecting Limoges boxes are Nancy Reagan and Morgan Fairchild. Singer and songwriter Elton John, whose love of flowers is legendary, has numerous porcelain boxes, including a number of Rochard pieces. Among his collection are, of course, many florals.

Collections can begin in a number of ways. Very often, a box is given as a gift to mark one of life's important events (from weddings to the birth of a new baby) or those ordinary events with deep, personal significance.

The interest grows from there. "It's the perfect kind of gift to start a collection with," says Annelle Guss, owner of the Beverly Hills emporium Francis-Orr, who has been carrying Rochard boxes in her store since their introduction. "And they are especially wonderful to collect because they don't take up an entire room."

Some enthusiasts stumbled upon these boxes by chance, in fine department stores, specialty shops and boutiques, as well as through mail-order catalogs. Other collectors were originally drawn to antique boxes—and perhaps have a few of their own—but their prices have risen in recent years, costing upward of $1,000 each. "Even the serious antique box collector probably finds some of the new ones charming and decorative," observes the Metropolitan's Mr. Curran.

Although most collectors are women, some Limoges enthusiasts are men. "We have several male collectors who love them and think they're wonderful," Mrs. Guss explains.

Limoges boxes, such as the wedding cake (right), are an increasingly popular gift registry item for brides-to-be.

Elton John displays his fine collection of Limoges boxes, many with floral themes,
some with lush bouquets (right) and others intertwined with violets (above).

One such collector is Michael Wayne, the eldest son of actor John Wayne, who is a movie producer and the head of an independent motion picture company. "I love 'em," he says of his collection, which numbers about 65 pieces. He has so many that he has stopped counting.

IT STARTED WITH A GIFT

Before he began collecting Limoges porcelain boxes himself, Mr. Wayne started giving them as gifts about 15 years ago. "I must have bought zillions as gifts," he muses. "I've given golf boxes to my son-in-law, who's very interested in golf. If we go to somebody's house for dinner and we want to take along a little something, we'll bring a box related to their hobby or interest. I've given a lot of animal boxes as gifts—especially cats," he adds. Mr. Wayne has bestowed boxes upon his mother and his four daughters as well as his wife, Gretchen. Many of his gifts have, in turn, spurred new collectors. "They're fairly priced, so you can afford to give them to people and to collect them yourself."

COLLECTING BY CATEGORY

Mr. Wayne began assembling his own collection about five years ago. Like many collectors, Mr. Wayne was first attracted to one category—appropriately, those with a Western motif. "I'm very interested in the West and the history of the West," he explains. Indian bonnets, cowboy hats and teepees dominate his collection, as well as cameras and any items related to the film industry. His other interests, travel and reading, are also reflected in boxes, as

well as his love for animals. He's got turkeys, roosters and several spaniels, inspired by a beloved family pet. "I just collect things that appeal to me, that are part of my life," Mr. Wayne says.

Two of Mr. Wayne's daughters, spurred by their father's gifts, have begun collecting by category: one, like her father, collects Western motifs; the other, fruits and vegetables.

"What I love is that they constantly come out with new and better styles. It makes me feel as if I've got to have them," he explains. "It's addictive."

Gretchen Wayne prefers to display her Limoges boxes directly on furniture, while her husband keeps his in glass cabinets—"so they're easier to maintain." Like most collectors, the Waynes tend to display their collection in its entirety, creating a breathtaking effect. But there are as many ways to display one's collection as there are boxes.

EXHIBITING EN MASSE

Eileen Minnick, a bank executive in Palm Beach, has amassed such a huge collection of Limoges porcelain boxes—475 in all—she had to purchase a large curio cabinet for her living room. A box lover, she first began collecting antique wooden ones, but found they were taking up too much space. When she stumbled upon a Limoges box at a friend's house about 15 years ago, she fell in love with it and knew this was one item she could collect in large numbers.

"I started collecting them as soon as they came out," Ms. Minnick recalls. "Sometimes

Frequent travelers, Ms. Minnick among them, are drawn to Rochard's endearing luggage boxes.

I'd buy five at a time." Once her cabinet was filled with about 400 pieces, she had to put up a shelf in the bathroom to display what she calls "my cats." Somehow, little boxes have managed to creep onto her living room mantel, which has become another exhibition space. "They start to take on a life of their own," Ms. Minnick explains.

Her first boxes were flowers, followed by travel, "because I do a lot of traveling." Then she started buying for the different seasons. Ms. Minnick has Nativity pieces, numerous Santas, as well as Easter and Halloween boxes. "I go crazy at Christmas and decorate every room of my house." Then she moved on to boxes with the little bottles inside and recently ordered a chess set. So extensive is her collection, it's difficult for friends to buy boxes for her without picking something she already has.

"I love the fact that you can pick them up and open them," Ms. Minnick explains. "They are great conversation pieces. Everybody recognizes them right away and asks about them. They are so detailed. They are really exquisite little things."

THE JOY OF DISPLAY

"I group them by category," says Candy Spelling, the wife of TV producer Aaron Spelling and a Beverly Hills philanthropist. Mrs. Spelling started collecting boxes around 1982, when she and her husband first moved into their enormous Beverly Hills mansion. "I bought them as accessories for tables in some of my rooms," she says. A few vegetables were acquired first; now her collection numbers about 200.

In a powder room she displays the boxes with perfume bottles inside; in a bedroom, a heart arrangement. In two cabinets in her bathroom are her favorites—butterflies and flowers—so she can see them everyday. "I like them all, what can I tell you?" she muses. "I keep saying I'm not going to buy any more and then they come out with some really cute ones and I can't resist."

Mrs. Spelling loves the way they're made. "They're just charming. I love the way the clasps have something to do with the motif, or sometimes there's a cute little painted something inside," she says. "There are a lot of copies out there but they don't have the same quality as the Limoges boxes."

Like the Waynes, Mrs. Spelling also enjoys giving the boxes as gifts. "They're the perfect gift for someone who has everything or when you can't find something for a man—there are the golf boxes, little fountain pens, globes and the tuxedo shirt. And they're all charming."

Tina Lowrie of San Francisco also groups her 130 pieces by theme and creates changing and seasonal displays. "Next to a picture of my nephew I have a little baseball box because he loves that sport," Ms. Lowrie explains. "And since my husband and I did a

Eileen Minnick's box collection numbers 475—at last count.

lot of our dating by phone there's a phone next to his photo."

In her library are boxes that relate to books. On her dressing table are her favorites: a rooster, a chess-set queen and a French "Santon" woman, a folk style from the South of France. In her office, a travel mélange includes an Eiffel tower, British bowler hat and a hatbox. There are boxes on shelves and boxes on furniture. In spring she displays flower boxes; in fall, a pumpkin; in winter, festive boxes that are hung from the tree as ornaments. "I rotate my boxes so it feels as if I have new ones," she explains. Ms. Lowrie became intrigued with the boxes when she began selling them in 1980. She still sells them and is still intrigued. "I like little boxes and well-made little things so I was already predisposed to like something like them," she explains. Her first intention was to collect only vegetables—"I loved the colors"—but her collection blossomed from there. Most of her boxes are Rochard.

AN ATTRACTION TO QUALITY

"Customers who collect know the difference," explains Mrs. Guss, who only sells Rochard boxes in her store. "The painting is so much better."

Beverly See of Goldens Bridge, New York, agrees. She had been drawn to the boxes after first seeing them in England. "They are of better quality. The painting, the clasp, the way you open the box—everything about them. I just kept being drawn to Rochard boxes."

Miss See has six boxes so far—her first was a Neiman Marcus shopping bag—but vows that's only the beginning. "I can't wait to get another piece."

As to the business of collecting, it can be difficult to find older pieces, perhaps because they have been around only since the late 1970s. The rarity of older pieces also demonstrates that collectors are not in the business of buying and selling their boxes; they hold on to them. Even when collectors die, their Limoges boxes rarely end up in estate sales or auctions. "I attend many auctions and estate sales and rarely do I see a Limoges box," Mr. Sonking adds. "This says one thing to me: that these boxes are so loved that they remain in the family and are passed down from generation to generation."

SELECTED BIBLIOGRAPHY

Banque De France et Sécrétariat Régional Du Limousin, L'Industrie Porcelainière En Limousin: Evolution récente et perspectives d'avenir. Limoges, Banque De France, 1995.

Balabanian, Olivier; Barrière, Bernadette; Cassan, Michel; Chambon, Guy; Robert, Maurice; Villoutreix, Marcel; Forces et Douceurs en Limousin Paris: Editions Christine Bonnefon, 1995.

Beauchamp-Markowsky, Barbara (French translation by Tamara Préaud). Boîtes En Porcelaine. Fribourg: Les Editions de L'Amateur, 1985.

Bedford, John, All Kinds of Small Boxes. New York: Walker, 1965.

Blakemore, Kenneth. Snuff Boxes. London: Frederick Muller Limited, 1976.

Blonston, Gary, "A Surprise in Every Box," Art & Antiques, February, 1995, 75-77.

Chassain, Pierre, Contes des Forêts et des Landes Limousines. Naves: Editions de la Veytizou, 1991.

Chatain, Georges, Le Limousin—Terre Sensible et Rebelle. Paris: Editions Autrement, 1995.

Chilton, Meredith, "Porcelain Boxes: Miniature Masterpieces of the Eighteenth Century," Antiques, April 1991, 764-773.

Comstock, Helen, "Collection of French Snuff Boxes, Connoisseur, June, 1949, 112.

Cooper-Hewitt Museum, Boxes: The Smithsonian Illustrated Library of Antiques. Washington, D.C., The Smithsonian Institution, 1982.

Corti, Egon Caesar, conte, (translated by Paul England), The History of Smoking . London: G.G. Harrap & Co., Ltd, 1931.

Couppey, Francoise and Barbarin, Bernard, Les Plus Belles Ballades en Limousin. Lyon: Les Créations du Pélican, 1994.

Cox, Warren E., The Book of Pottery and Porcelain. New York: Crown Publishers, Inc., 1970.

Curtis, Mattoon, M., The Book of Snuff and Snuff Boxes. New York: Liveright Publishing Corporation, 1935.

Cushon, J.P., Animals in Pottery and Porcelain. London: Cory Adams & MacKay, 1966.

D'Albis, Jean (translated by L. D'Albis), Haviland. Paris: Dessain et Tolra, 1988.

David, Martine and Delrieu, Anne-Marie. Aux Sources des Chansons Populaires. Collection le Français Retrouvé. Paris: Belin, 1984.

Decoux-Lagoutte, Edouard, Un Coin du Limousin. Tulle: Traditions, 1883.

Eriksen, Svend, Sèvres Porcelain: Vincennes and Sèvres, 1740-1800. London: Faber and Faber, 1987.

Dugue, Charles (Christine Bonnichon, ed., Fêtes et Gâteaux. Artigues-près-Bordeaux: Imprimerie Delmas, 1981, p. 84.

Fay-Halle, Antoinette (translated by Barbara Mundt), Porcelain of the Nineteenth Century. New York: Rizzoli, 1983.

Ferniot, Jean, French Regional Cooking, New York: Crescent Books, 1991.

Foursaud, Albert, La Société Rurale Traditionelle en Limousin, 1976.

Fourest, Henry-Pierre, "Les Boîtes En Porcelaine Tendre," Cahiers de la Céramique et des Arts du Feu #13, April 21, 1959, 44-51.

Frantz, Henri, French Pottery & Porcelain. New York: Charles Scribner's Sons, 1906.

Garnier, Edouard, The Soft Paste Porcelain of Sèvres. Paris: Booking International, 1988.

Gasnault, Paul, French Pottery. London: Chapman & Hall Limited, 1884.

Gaston, Mary Frank, The Collector's Encyclopedia of Limoges Porcelain. Paducah: Collectors Books, 1992.

Godden, Geoffrey A, Godden's Guide to European Porcelain. London: Barrie & Jenkins, 1993.

Jacquemart, Albert, (translated by Mrs. Bury Palliser), History of the Ceramic Art. New York: Scribner, Armstrong & Co., 1877.

Johnson, Bruce E., "Pottery & Porcelain," Country Living, November, 1995, 41-42.

Jones, Colin, Cambridge Illustrated History of France. Cambridge: Cambridge University Press, 1994.

Keefe, John W., "The Porcelains of Paris," Antiques, February, 1996, 283-291.

Lacan, Claude, Limoges Mémoire. Saint-Etienne: Edi Loire, 1996.

Latham, Jean, Collecting Miniature Antiques. New York: Scribner, 1972.

Le Corbellier, Clare, European & American Snuff Boxes. London: Chancellor Press, 1966.

Lewer, H.W., The Bric-à-Brac Collector. London: Herbert Jenkins Limited, 1923.

Massignon, Genevieve, ed., Folktales of France. Chicago: University of Chicago Press, 1968.

Meister, Peter Wilhelm (translated by Ewald Osers), European Porcelain of the 18th Century. Ithaca: Cornell University Press, 1983.

Merriman, John M., The Red City: Limoges and the French Nineteenth Century. Oxford: Oxford University Press, 1985.

The Metropolitan Museum of Art, Enamels of Limoges. New York: The Metropolitan Museum of Art, 1996.

Molière (translated by Christopher Hampton), Don Juan,. London: Faber and Faber, 1974.

Musée Des Arts Decoratifs, Animaux-Boîtes. Paris: Réunion Des Musées Nationaux, 1992.

Meslin-Perrier, Chantal, National Museum of Adrien Dubouché. Limoges: Albin Michel, for Musées et Monuments de France, 1992.

Owens, Mitchell, "Works of Art That Once Humbly Bore the Soup," The New York Times, March 2, 1997, 41.

Perouas, Louis, Histoire de Limoges. Toulouse: Editions Privas, 1989.

Peyramaure, Michel, Le Limousin. Rennes: Ouest France, 1993.

Propert, John Lumsden, A History of Miniature Art. London: MacMillon & Co., 1887.

Robert, Maurice, Le Guide de la Haute-Vienne. Lyon: Editions de la Manufacture, 1995.

Rollins, Alice R., "Snuff & Patch Boxes of Another Day," California Art & Architecture, December, 1932, 4.

Root, Waverly, The Food of France. New York: Vintage Books, 1966.

Schmidt, R., (translated by W.A. Thorpe), Porcelain as an Art and as a Mirror of Fashion. London: G.G. Harrap & Co., Ltd., 1932.

SEMA 20, Le Limousin Métiers D'Art, St. Léonard de Noblat: Imprimerie Montibus, 1996.

Snowman, Kenneth, "A Second Pinch of the Snuff," Magazine Antiques, January, 1990, 300-307.

Stock, Marie Lena, "A Retailer's Guide to Porcelain Boxes," Gifts & Decorative Accessories, February, 1996, 83-88.

Tindall, Gillian, "The Country Airs and Graces of Limoges," The New York Times, March 10, 1996, 8-9, 29.

Turner, Jane, Ed., Dictionary of Art. London: Macmillan Publishers Limited, 1996.

Verynaud, Georges, Limoges—Si ma Ville m'était Contée. Limoges: Centre Régional De Documentation, 1988.

Weiss, Gustav (translated by Janet Seligman), The Book of Porcelain. New York: Praeger Publishers, 1971.

Worthington, Christa, "From Royalty's Best Friend to Collectors' Favorite," The New York Times, February 8, 1998, 35.

Wyckoff, Elizabeth, Dry Drunk: The Culture of Tobacco in 17th- and 18th-century Europe. New York: The New York Public Library, Astor, Lenox and Tilden Foundations, 1997.

PHOTO CREDITS

Photography copyright © Freddy Le Saux, pages: 2-3, 21, 35, 36, 40, 41, 42, 43, 45, 88, 94, 96, 97, 98 (top), 100, 108, 110, 113, 114-117, 119-123, 127, 130, 131, 133, 135, 141, 146, 149, 150, 152, 153, 154-165, 166, 168-176.

Photography copyright © George Ross, pages: 3 (butterfly), 8, 11, 12, 13, 15, 19, 24, 27, 28, 31, 49, 52, 55, 58, 62 (lower right, 63 (lower right), 64, 65 (lower right), 66, 67 (top), 68 (lower right), 69, 70, 72, 73, 76, 80, 81, 82, 84, 85, 86, 90, 95, 99, 102, 103, 104, 106, 107, 111, 124, 125, 126 (top), 128, 132, 134, 136, 138-140, 144, 147, 148, 151, 177, 178, 181-187, 190 (lower right), 191-203, 205, 207-209, 210 (top), 211, 217, 218, 219 (upper left, lower right, middle), 220, 223, 227-230, 233.

Photography copyright © Dylan Cross, pages: 68, 77, 188, 189, 212-216, 219 (lower left), 221.

Photography copyright © Mort Kaye, page: 231.

Illustrations copyright © Julia Grant, pages: 145, 153.

Illustrations by Jean-Luc Soulat, pages: 166-172, 174-176.

Oil paintings on canvas by Christopher McCall, pages: 5, 8, 233. Mr. McCall is a native New Yorker currently residing in Bucks County Pennsylvania. His expressive oil paintings portray the essence of floral and still life painting. A Limoges box will often be the subject, or part of, Mr. McCall's compositions. His paintings have been exhibited nationally and can be found in numerous private and corporate collections throughout the United States and abroad.

Product styling: Ron Prybycien & Karin Strom

Research in France: Marie Annik Luirette-Boussarie

Technical advisor in France: Christian Lebois

Museum pieces:

p. 16: squatting chinaman snuff box, Limoges, Musée Adrien Dubouché, copyright © Photo RMN; p. 17: Marco Polo Arriving in China, Corbis-Bettmann; p. 20: double barrel box decorated with flowers, Bruxelles, Musées royaux d'Art et d'Histoire - Inv. # SY. 119; p. 23: heart-shaped box, Limoges, Musée Adrien Dubouché, copyright © Photo-Magnoux; p. 25: monk-shaped box, Musée des Arts décoratifs, Paris, photo Laurent-Sully Jaulmes, tous droits réservés, Fev. 98; p. 25: cat-shaped box, Musée des Arts décoratifs, Paris, photo Laurent-Sully Jaulmes, tous droits réservés, Fev. 98; p. 26: cat-shaped snuff box, Limoges, Musée Adrien Dubouché, copyright © Photo-Magnoux; p. 26: couple in bed, Bruxelles, Musées royaux d'Art et d'Histoire - Inv. # SY. 152; p. 29: horse-shaped box, Limoges, Musée Adrien Dubouché, copyright © Photo RMN; p. 29: swan-shaped snuff box, Limoges, Musée Adrien Dubouché, copyright © Photo-Magnoux; p. 33: portrait of Monsieur Darnet, Anonymous, Limoges, Musée Adrien Dubouché, copyright © Photo RMN; p. 37: Turgot coat of arms, Limoges, Musée Adrien Dubouché, copyright © Photo RMN;

p. 43: aerial view of La Seynie porcelain factory, historic photo from La Reine factory archives; p. 44: part of the original La Seynie factory building, historic photo from La Reine factory archives; p. 46: Royal Profile Portrait of King Louis XIV, Corbis-Bettmann; p. 48: Portrait of Louis XV, Corbis-Bettmann; p. 48: King Louis XVI of France, Leonard de Selva/Corbis; p. 51: Formal Portrait of Catherine de Medici, Corbis-Bettmann; p. 53: "Dugazon, dans Sganarelle du Festin de Pierre," hand colored etching, from Petite Galerie Dramatique, ou Recueil de differents costumes acteurs des theatres de la Capitale, published by Martinet, Paris, 1800 (MEM+ J77 jpo), Print Collection, Miriam and Ira D. Wallach Division of Art, Prints and Photographs, The New York, Public Library, Astor, Lenox and Tilden Foundations; p. 56: J'ai du bon Tabac, Vielles Chansons et Rondes de M. Boutet de Monvel; p. 60: Paintings, French, Pecheux: Maria Luisa of Parma..., The Metropolitan Museum of Art, Bequest of Annie C. Kane, 1926, (26.260.9), Photograph copyright © 1995 The Metropolitan Museum of Art; p. 61: dog box, Limoges, Musée Adrien Dubouché, copyright © Photo RMN - Hervé Lewandowski; Paintings, French, Pecheux: Maria Luisa of Parma...(DETAIL), The Metropolitan Museum of Art, Bequest of Annie C. Kane, 1926, (26.260.9), Photograph copyright © 1995 The Metropolitan Museum of Art; p. 62 (left): hunter-shaped box, Musée des Arts décoratifs, Paris, photo Laurent-Sully Jaulmes, tous droits réservés; p. 63 (left): nun-shaped box, Musée des Arts décoratifs, Paris, photo Laurent-Sully Jaulmes, tous droits réservés, Fev. 98; p. 65 (top): box in the shape of a girl's head with a mask, Museum für Kunst und Gewerbe Hamburg, Sammlung Blohm; p. 65 (lower left): shoe-shaped box, Limoges, Musée Adrien Dubouché, copyright © Photo-Magnoux; p. 67 (bottom): chinoiseries style box, Copenhagen Kunstindustrimuseum - Inv. # B 249/1939; p. 68 (lower left): double box, Bruxelles, Musées royaux d'art et d'histoire - Inv. # SY.81; p. 71: Formal Portrait of Napoleon, Corbis-Bettmann; p. 74: Pastoral Scene by Francois Boucher, Alexander Burkatowski/Corbis; p. 75: lamb box, Limoges, Musée Adrien Dubouché, copyright © Photo RMN - Hervé Lewandowski; p. 78: bonbonnière with feet of rocaille, Limoges, Musée Adrien Dubouché, copyright © Photo RMN - Magnoux; p. 83: Portrait of Madame de Pompadour, Library of Congress/Corbis; p. 87: A Description of the Military Carriage..., London, 1816, title page and folded frontispiece (Arents S 0941), Arents Collection, The New York Public Library, Astor, Lenox and Tilden Foundation; p. 91: aerial view of porcelain factory buildings print, Chastagner factory archives; p. 93: Vienne River print, Chastagner factory archives; p. 98 (bottom): La Reine's first collection of whiteware, La Reine factory archives; p. 101: porcelain workers firing kiln print, Chastagner factory archives; p. 118 (top): interior view of central hall at the Musée Adrien Dubouché, copyright © Photo RMN; p. 118 (bottom left): interior view of the Musée Adrien Dubouché, copyright © Photo RMN; p. 179: figure of a woman box, Limoges, Musée Adrien Dubouché, copyright © Photo RMN - Magnoux; p. 180: walnut-shaped box, Limoges, Musée Adrien Dubouché, copyright © Photo RMN - Magnoux; p. 204 (top left): drum-shaped box, Copenhagen Kunstindustrimuseum - Inv. # B 21/1939; pp. 224 & 225: Elton John Flower Fantasies, Weidenfeld & Nicolson Ltd., Andrew Twort.

ACKNOWLEDGMENTS

We gratefully acknowledge the dedication to this project from the following individuals:
Dottie Adams, Christy Archer, Clover Archer, Patrick Audevard, Danièle Baudrier, Marie Annik Luirette-Boussarie, Mady & Gérard Chastagner, Alain Cloarec, John Curran, Josie Dimatulac, Steven Donelian, Anne Étot, Leonard Florence, Joanne Furio, Deirdre Gallagher, Julia Grant, Sarah Grant, Annelle Gus, Peter Hurst, Mort Kaye, Hiroko Küffner, Nancy Knott, Jean-Louis Lacroix, Christian Lebois, Clare LeCorbellier, Yvette Leighton, Freddie Le Saux, Paul Marquet, Jean-Paul Marquet, Carol Maurielo, Christopher McCall, Chantal Meslin-Perrier, Eileen Minnick, Dr. Genelle Morain, Annie Pichard, Ron Prybycien, Gérard Ribierre, George Ross, Samantha Scully, André Sibinski, Jean-Luc Soulat, Candy Spelling, Mary Ellen Statlander, Karen Strom, Liz Trovato, Cynthia Vasques, Mitch Wasserman, Fred Watson, Michael Wayne

COLLECTORS SOURCE LIST

p. 3: PV-587, large butterfly; **p. 7:** MC-849, typewriter; **p. 8:** PV-555, grandfather clock; AD-147, books; RA-335, open book; AB-448, turkey; **p. 11:** PV-589, basket of forget-me-nots; **p. 12:** hearts-RA-159, PV-283, NS-181, AD-136, AD-131, RA-412, MC-745, CM-080, RSC-673; **p. 13:** RA-347, purse; **p. 15:** PV-456, apple; **p. 19:** PV-227, oval box with relief floral basket; **p. 22:** PC-124, flat gold heart; **p. 24:** LA-128, cat box; **p. 27:** AB-419, Mr. & Mrs. St. Denis; **p. 28:** AB-410, large horse; **p. 30:** PV-680, tea warmer; **p. 38:** MC-729, postcard; **p. 49:** balloons - NS-164, RA-240, NS-163 **p. 52:** AD-175, cubano cigar; 663-2C, ashtray; AD-172, single cigar; AD-173, box of cigars **p. 55:** MC-729, wish you were here box; RA-375, black pen; RA-399, memories box ; MC-788, thinking of you envelope; RA-409,brown pen; **p. 57:** PV-603, mandolin box; **p. 58:** RA-230, round mirrored compact; **p. 59:** PV-267, shell; PV-307, shell; **p. 62:** MC-003, hunter; **p. 63:** MC-004, nun; **p. 64:** PV-410, doll's head; **p. 65:** PV-241, shoe shape with insect pattern; **p. 66:** RA-324, chair with book; NS-416, armoire; **p. 67:** CO-106, oval box; **p. 68:** CY-104, double box; **p. 69:** PV-461, rosebud; MC-737, canister; MC-734, egg; MC-736, chest; MC-735, rectangular; MC-733, heart ; **p. 70:** TB-001, drum; **p. 72:** 98-018, flat briquette; **p. 73:** PV-468, lily; DC-132, amaryllis; PV-459, lily ; **p. 76:** PV-311, basket with heart back; **p. 77:** PV-655, box with perfume bottles; **p. 79:** AD-400, chess set; **p. 80:** MC-882, antique camera; **p. 81:** AB-134, fish; AB-200, fish; AB-122, fish; **p. 82:** AB-046, pug box; **p. 84:** SW-073, double-sided box; **p. 85:** MC-970, envelope with note; **p. 86:** PV-224, heart; **p. 90:** AD-164, globe; **p. 95:** PV-656, wicker trunk; **p. 102:** NS-368, Arc de Triomphe; LA-105, Eiffel Tower; **p. 103:** 80-016, cobalt egg with bottle; 80-060, cobalt basket with bottles; **p. 104:** NS-256, watercolors; PV-684, yellow paint tube; PV-703, green paint tube; PV-682, red paint tube; PV-683, blue paint tube; **p. 106:** NS-213, hat pin box; RA-341, thimble box; NS-257, thimble box; **p. 107:** TR-107, soap; **p. 111:** RA-406, round luggage; RA-405, suitcase; **p. 124:** MC-925, shoe box with shoes; PV-710, Paris shoe box with shoes; MC-926, shoe box with shoes; **p. 125:** LG-175, wine cask; PV-671, wine crate with bottles; **p. 126:** NS-324, glove box; PV-305, round basket; PV-222, double basket; **p. 128:** RA-303, cookbook; RA-423, crepe cookbook; RA-447, cookbook with rolling pin; **p. 129:** PV-606, clafoutis; PV-593, clafoutis slice; **p. 132:** AD-149, soup tureen and platter; PV-673, foie gras; **p. 134:** RA-277, witch; **p. 136:** PV-236, oblong box; **p. 138:** MC-700, black telephone; MC-935, floral telephone; NS-395, mini telephone; **p. 139:** MC-941, candy heart; RA-390, flower box; MC-769, hanging heart; **p. 140:** RA-378, egg carton; **p. 142:** AB-400, partridge; AB-424, yorkie; AB-401, fish; CW-024, oval; CW-028, heart; **p. 143:** AB-418, owl; AB-415, cat; AB-403, three monkeys; CW-010, egg; CW-016, octagonal; CV-06, apple; **p. 144:** PV-738, apple; **p. 147:** CT-04, pear tapestry; CT-06, apple tapestry; CW-06, apple strawberry; CW-028, strawberry heart; CV-06, pear shasta daisy; CW-028, heart strawberry; **p. 148:** AD-201, black bottom pig; **p. 151:** MC-702, birdhouse; **p. 177:** RSC-631, cherry box; **p. 178:** DC-101, champagne in bucket; **p. 181:** PV-226, walnut with insect pattern; **p. 182:** AB-413, large frog; RA-173, lilypad; AB-015, frog; **p. 183:** AB-145. bird with babies; **p. 184:** AB-174. bunny; **p. 185:** AB-195, panda; **p. 186:** NS-180, flat octagonal box; **p. 187:** AD-143, Victoria & Albert Museum rose box reproduction; **p. 188:** RA-411, egg; RA-412, heart; **p. 189:** AD-104, traditional shape with fruit painting; **p. 190:** 98-013, egg with thimble; NS-385, Noah's Ark; MC-839, dreidel; **p. 191:** RA-432, hat box; **p. 192:** NS-298, picnic basket; PV-708, straw-berry basket; **p. 193:** NS-444, chateau; **p. 194:** PV-481, hand with glove; **p. 195:** RA-315, jack-o-lantern; **p. 196:** NS-384, scales; **p. 197:** DC-106, alarm clock; **p. 198:** RA-116, red chili pepper; PV-572, apple; **p. 199:** MC-750, red bell pepper; RA-241, eggplant; MC-756, avocado; PV-521, Italian green pepper; PV-313, garlic; RA-113, large green bell pepper; PV-316, carrot; MC-751, mini green bell pepper; PV-567, mini carrot; **p. 200:** AB-197, pig & snail on see-saw; **p. 201:** NS-435, toy chest; **p. 202:** LA-119, tooth fairy; **p. 203:** PV-660, Russian doll; **p. 204:** AB-009, violin; **p. 205:** PV-408, piano; PV-523, violin & case; **p. 206:** NS-427, jumping horse; NS-157, tennis racquet; **p. 207:** TR-100, golf ball; MC-974, golf club; **p. 208:** AB-045, snail; PV-546, ladybug; PV-713, flower & butterfly; PV-444, poppy; **p. 209:** PV-472, yellow lily; **p. 210:** EV-102, orange marmalade; RA-357, frying pan; RA-371, toaster; RA-377, cheese dome; **p. 211:** NS-151, coffee grinder; PV-609, coffee cup; NS-387, coffee bean bag; **p. 212:** RSC-672, oval "magnolia"; RSC-630, rectangle "oranges"; **p. 213:** RSC-730, footed "women's scarf"; RSC-840, shaped "the violin"; **p. 214:** RSC-757, oval "bathing blue birds"; RSC-673, heart "three tulips"; RSC-765, empire sofa; **p. 215:** RSC-913, oval "cherubs"; RSC-621, rectangle "remember me"; RSC-740, octagonal "regal cat"; **p. 216:** RSC-701, octagonal "Father Christmas"; RSC-703, shaped "brown breasted newlyweds"; RSC-813, oval "the sleigh"; **p. 217:** MC-994, egg with butterfly; RA-320, emperor's palace; NS-238, fu-dog; PR-100, Buddha; **p. 218:** NS-378, Cinderella carriage; **p. 219:** PV-403, peasant woman; NS-388, teacart (with detail); NS-352, canister shape; **p. 220:** PV-542, egg with bottle; **p. 221:** PV-461, rosebud; PV-463, dogwood; PV-468, lily; **p. 222:** NS-408, baby carriage; NS-366, pacifier; **p. 223:** RA-309, wedding cake; **p. 226:** RA-198, tepee; PV-561, cowboy boot; MC-820, saquato cactus; **p. 227:** PV-549, western hat; RA-499, suitcase; **p. 228:** RA-421, nutcracker; **p. 229:** RA-297, Victorian Santa; **p. 230:** RA-321, angel; RA-349, double angel; **p. 232:** AD-147, books; RA-274, book with glasses; RA-335, open book.

MUSEUM COLLECTIONS

Decorative boxes, including those used for snuff, can be found in the museums around the world. The following is a list of some of the best-known collections:

United States

Chicago: The Art Institute of Chicago
New York: The Metropolitan Museum of Art, Cooper-Hewitt Museum
Philadelphia: Philadelphia Museum of Art
Washington, DC: Smithsonian Institute

Europe

Berlin: Kunstgewerbemuseum
Limoges: The Adrien Dubouché Museum
Paris: Musée des Arts Décoratifs
London: Victoria and Albert Museum
Vienna: Kunsthistorisches Museum

INDEX